The March On Russia

A play

David Storey

Samuel French – London
New York – Sydney – Toronto – Hollywood

Copyright © 1989 by David Storey
All Rights Reserved

THE MARCH ON RUSSIA is fully protected under the copyright laws of the British Commonwealth, including Canada, the United States of America, and all other countries of the Copyright Union. All rights, including professional and amateur stage productions, recitation, lecturing, public reading, motion picture, radio broadcasting, television and the rights of translation into foreign languages are strictly reserved.

ISBN 978-0-573-01698-1

www.samuelfrench.co.uk
www.samuelfrench.com

For Amateur Production Enquiries

United Kingdom and World
excluding north america
plays@samuelfrench.co.uk
020 7255 4302/01

Each title is subject to availability from Samuel French,
depending upon country of performance.

CAUTION: Professional and amateur producers are hereby warned that *THE MARCH ON RUSSIA* is subject to a licensing fee. Publication of this play does not imply availability for performance. Both amateurs and professionals considering a production are strongly advised to apply to the appropriate agent before starting rehearsals, advertising, or booking a theatre. A licensing fee must be paid whether the title is presented for charity or gain and whether or not admission is charged.

The Professional Rights in this play are controlled by United Agents LLP, Lexington House, 12-26 Lexington St, Soho, London W1F 0LE.

No one shall make any changes in this title for the purpose of production. No part of this book may be reproduced, stored in a retrieval system, or transmitted in any form, by any means, now known or yet to be invented, including mechanical, electronic, photocopying, recording, videotaping, or otherwise, without the prior written permission of the publisher. No one shall upload this title, or part of this title, to any social media websites.

The right of David Storey to be identified as author of this work has been asserted in accordance with Section 77 of the Copyright, Designs and Patents Act 1988.

THE MARCH ON RUSSIA

First presented by the National Theatre Company in the Lyttelton auditorium of the National Theatre on 6th April, 1989, with the following cast of characters:

Colin	Frank Grimes
Pasmore	Bill Owen
Mrs Pasmore	Constance Chapman
Wendy	Rosemary Martin
Eileen	Patsy Rowlands
Postman	Michael Goldie

The play was directed by Lindsay Anderson
Designed by Jocelyn Herbert

The action of the play takes place in the Pasmores' bungalow

Time—the present

ACT I	Scene 1	Three a.m.
	Scene 2	Morning
ACT II	Scene 1	Evening
	Scene 2	Next morning

CHARACTERS

Colin
Pasmore
Mrs Pasmore
Wendy
Eileen

ACT I

Scene 1

The Pasmores' bungalow. Three a.m.

We see the living room and kitchen of the bungalow, linked by a passage. There are three doors leading off the passage—to Pasmore's room (bedroom 1), Mrs Pasmore's room (bedroom 2) and the bathroom. An exit leads to the front door and there are stairs leading to the dormer bedroom

The rooms are furnished to suit the requirements of a retired working-class couple with affluent offspring, i.e., whilst retaining their own taste the contents of both interiors are in a much-used but good condition

There is the usual furniture in the living room together with an open fireplace and a window looking on to the street. The kitchen is furnished with units, a table (covered with a cloth), stools, an electric stove (with practical hob light and clock), fridge (switched on so it illuminates when opened), washing machine and sink with practical tap. There is a door to the rear garden

When the CURTAIN *rises it is dark. The coal fire has been allowed to die down but the coals still illuminate the room. A glow from behind the drawn curtains of the window suggests a night-time illumination from a road outside*

Colin, in pyjamas and dressing-gown, descends the stairs conscious of the silence of the house. He is middle-aged, early fifties, and stocky.

He goes into the kitchen, closing the door behind him, and switches on the hob light. He fills the kettle at the sink and plugs it in. He gets the teapot and a teabag, putting the latter into the former and milk from the fridge

A light goes on in bedroom 1, then goes out again. A moment later the door opens and Pasmore comes out. He is small, with a stocky figure, in his late eighties. He has preserved, however, a youthful apearance, if slow in movement. This is characterised by the formal way he does his hair, cut short and parted, with a fringe, and a figure which, as yet, hasn't gone to fat, despite his robust proportions. He, too, is dressed in pyjamas and dressing-gown

He feels his way to the kitchen. He coughs as he moves, clearing congestion, quietly so. He opens the kitchen door

Pasmore You up?
Colin I hope I didn't wake you.
Pasmore I'm often up in the night.
Colin Do you want a pot of tea?

Pasmore I wouldn't mind. (*He sits on the stool by the table*) Keeps me going. (*He has an abstracted look, as if he himself has been awake some time: incurious, reflective*) Once your mother's taken her pills it's as much as she can do to wake in the morning. It was a great surprise you coming. Done me and her a lot of good. (*He coughs*)

Colin sets another cup—his father's—on the table and puts a tea-bag into it

Are you warm enough up theer?
Colin All right.
Pasmore These dormer bedrooms weren't really designed for these bungalows. They had 'em put in later when the houses didn't sell. (*He rises to move the curtain at the kitchen window*) Moors at the back, farm fields at the front. Sea a mile off. (*He breathes in*) Salt air. Kept me alive. That and a good wife. It's paid its way, you buying this house. How long has it to run on the mortgage?
Colin Five years. (*He makes the tea*)
Pasmore Better keep us voices down. (*He takes his cup*) What time is it? (*He goes to the kitchen door*)

Colin stoops to look at the clock on the stove

Colin Three o'clock.
Pasmore Can get world news.
Colin Hear it tomorrow.
Pasmore Right. (*As he goes*) Better put the milk back.
Colin Right.
Pasmore Goes off if you leave it out.

Colin, having completed his own cup of tea, puts out the light over the stove, recovers the milk and puts it back in the fridge

Pasmore, entering the living-room, goes directly to the fire, stoops, coughs, picks up the poker, re-ignites the ashes. Colin follows, closing the door, and is about to put the light on

No: that 'un.

Colin puts on the reading lamp

Good coal.
Colin It ought to be.
Pasmore Aye (*He straightens up*)
Colin You've dug it long enough.
Pasmore T'on'y collier round here, tha knows. All farmer's men. One or two schoolteachers. A dozen work at the radar station, up on Kielty Moor. Go past it in the car. Not a sign o' bloody life. Two hundred and fifty people work there, round the clock, twenty-four hours a day, three hundred and sixty-five days in the year. When it snows they sleep in bunkers. Watches Russia. (*He coughs*) How long did it take you to drive up?
Colin Five hours. (*He sits*)

Act I, Scene 1

Pasmore A car like that. Do over a hundred, can't it?
Colin A bit.
Pasmore I bet! (*He has taken a seat himself*) How long are you up for?
Colin A couple of days.
Pasmore We allus hope it'll be a bit longer.
Colin All I can manage.
Pasmore How are your kiddies?
Colin Fine.
Pasmore Kay?
Colin Terrific!

Pasmore laughs

Pasmore Married how long?
Colin Twenty-nine years.
Pasmore Takes some beating.
Colin It does!
Pasmore A good wife. Home. Children. I don't know what else it's all about.
Colin No.

Pause

Pasmore Put ought i' my cup she'd twig it i' the morning. "Have you been drinking?"! Drinking! (*He laughs*)
Colin Get up once in the night or often?
Pasmore Nay, up and down, in and out. Sometimes up once, then back. I rarely get to sleep afore three or four.
Colin You were tonight.
Pasmore How could you tell?
Colin I heard you snoring.
Pasmore Not me, old lad.
Colin Sounded to come from below.
Pasmore Your mother.
Colin I remember that at home! (*He laughs*)
Pasmore Bennetts' one side, Cliftons' the other. Remember their dog? Gev us no sleep a night or two.
Colin The one next door isn't much improvement.
Pasmore Sheepdog. Keep it penned up. *He* works at the radar station. Hasn't much time for a dog. (*He cocks his head to listen*) Can sometimes hear one of their lads playing electronic music. The walls o' these houses aren't that thick.
Colin Does it keep you awake?
Pasmore Can't grumble. Other people have bigger worries. What have you been doing?
Colin Working.
Pasmore Ought to take a rest.
Colin I do from time to time.
Pasmore I sometimes wonder if I haven't dreamt half the things I've done. Like living where we were afore: pit ten streets off, shop, pub, picture-

house at the corner: I wek up at night and still think I can hear the dynamo, smell that smoke. Never late once, in forty-five years.
Colin Some record.
Pasmore In the first twenty years, if I had a week off I had to work sixteen hours each day the week afore. It takes some beating.
Colin It does.
Pasmore When I went back, afore we moved here. I f'und three men doing the job I'd done. Pit deputy, tha knows. (*Pause*) I sometimes hear Bennett going down that path. He died twenty-five years ago. "Standing around all day", I'd tell him, "i' front of a bloody furnace." He wa're a steam locomotive driver, though when I first knew him he drove a hoss and cart. Worked for Bullcliff's, the farmer and coalmerchant. Had bell-pits on his land. That's the time of your mother's father. He used to do his hosses. How's Kay?
Colin You've asked me.
Pasmore And the children?
Colin Fine.
Pasmore All earning their living.
Colin Just about.
Pasmore (*leaning forward; poking the fire*) Your sister Wendy's getting divorced.
Colin I know.
Pasmore Your sister Eileen isn't much better. I've two daughters, both been married twenty-odd year, one wi' two kiddies, the other wi' none, and they've both gev up on their husbands.
Colin I thought Arnold gave up on Wendy.
Pasmore Since she became a politician she's had no time for family life. They were going to adopt two kiddies. That went out of the window. In my day you struggled through these problems. You didn't give in after two or three year.
Colin They've been married over twenty.
Pasmore We've been married fifty-nine. Sixty years tomorrow.
Colin Today.
Pasmore Today!
Colin Here's to it! (*He toasts Pasmore with his cup of tea*)
Pasmore Watch that every night. (*He indicates the television*) Destruction. People killing one another. Child molesting. Rape. Starvation.
Colin Wasn't it like that when you were young?
Pasmore Nay, got sent to Russia. Gev a false age. Invaded the Crimea. Set off from Sebastopol. We'd reached Rostov-on-Don when they decided we'd march back again. I wa're in the Royal Naval Air Service. Inducted at Gosport. Given six weeks training then taken out, at night, in a launch, wi' another lad, into the English Channel. Fu'st, out of nowhere, came a searchlight, then—out of the darkness—came a voice. "Pull alongside. Port beam." Ship plunging up and down. Ladder swinging from side to side, then out and in. Waves higher than this house. Half drowned. In the end they lowered a net. Dumped on deck. Know the first words I heard when I reported for duty in the Royal Navy? "Take that man's name fo'

Act I, Scene 1   5

spitting on the deck." Know what it wa'? A merchant-ship, with the superstructure taken off. The *Ark Royal*. The first aircraft-carrier in the world.

Colin What was your job?

Pasmore Patching planes. Made of wood and canvas. Put your foot in the wrong place and you went clean through. (*He laughs, coughs, then drinks his cooling tea*) Crossed the Bay of Biscay. Gibraltar: entered the Mediterranean. Stopped at Taranto, at the foot of Italy, a big Italian naval base. Cruised across the Ionian Sea to the Peloponnese. Crossed the Aegean, past Macedonia, through the Dardanelles, and entered the Black Sea. We anchored off the mouth of the Danube, then we sailed to Odessa. Took on a Russian General. Denisov. He had uniformed officers and courtiers with him. Crying when he came aboard. When he spoke to his wife he spoke in English. It was the height of the Revolution. Orders came from Winston Churchill. "Save the Tsar!" We set off from Sebastopol. Fighting Reds. Worst of all, starving groups of women. Some had guns but most had pitchforks, shovels, knives and axes. Used to come at night, in hordes. After the food. Couldn't stop them. Kill anybody that tried. We had marines, Gurkhas, and infantry. We fought all the way to Rostov-on-Don. Six hundred miles. Then we fought all the way back again. When we reached Sebastopol we were told to ditch the aircraft — stores, spares, the lot — and take on refugees. We filled up the holds with men, women and children. Lots of them had jewels. One woman with jewels round her neck, her fingers and her toes, asked me if I'd marry her.

Colin Perhaps you should.

Pasmore Nay, thy'd be a different cup of tea if I had! (*He laughs*)

Colin What happened after that?

Pasmore Took them to Constantinople. The Turkish authorities wouldn't let them ashore until they'd been deloused. Stripped 'em down: men and boys in one hold, women and girls in the other. Sprayed 'em down with hoses. Then a tender came out and took them off. After that we had to disinfect the ship, spray oursens, then, dive in off the stern, stark naked, and swim round to a ladder i' the bows. Sailed to Alexandria. We built an aerodrome at Abu Suar, out in the Egyptian desert. Played hockey. Boxed. Came home, sailing a torpedoed ship to Liverpool. I ended up in a Canadian air-force base in Lincolnshire, dismantling aeroplane engines. Then I came out. Within a year I wa' down the pit. Then I married. Had Eileen. You. Then Wendy. Forty-five years i' the coal-bin! A retirement home at the seaside. (*He coughs and reaches for the cup*) Do you want another cup of tea?

Colin I'll get one.

Colin takes his cup and goes to the kitchen. He puts the light on over the stove and plugs in the kettle.

A light goes on behind the second bedroom door. There is the noise of a chair being knocked inside. A few moments later Mrs Pasmore comes out. She wears a dressing-gown, and walks with a walking-stick. She is stout, but not plump, white-haired and in her eighties

Mrs Pasmore Tom?
Colin It's me, Mother.
Mrs Pasmore What're you doing up at this time?
Colin Couldn't sleep. Dad's up as well.

In the living-room Pasmore hastily rises, tidies the rug in front of the fire, the chair-cover and the cushion. Resumes his position

   Do you want a cup of tea?
Mrs Pasmore If you're making one. Is it cold up there?
Colin It's fine. The fire's lit in the living-room. Why don't you go in and keep warm?
Mrs Pasmore Well, if you're all right. (*She goes into the living-room*)
Pasmore Congratulations, love. (*He rises*)
Mrs Pasmore What's that?
Pasmore Sixty years. (*He kisses her cheek*)
Mrs Pasmore It's only three o'clock.
Pasmore Just after.
Mrs Pasmore We didn't get married until midday.
Pasmore Past midnight. Sixty years. (*Raising his voice to direct this to the kitchen*) I don't regret a minute.

Colin raises his head and smiles, making tea

Mrs Pasmore It's a bit late if you did. (*She looks at the clock on the mantelpiece*) This has stopped. You forgot to wind it.
Pasmore So I did. So I did. (*To Colin in the kitchen*) A night like this. (*To Mrs Pasmore*) Must want the time to go back'ards, love. (*He pokes the fire*)
Mrs Pasmore Put a bit of coal on, if you want it to blaze.
Pasmore Your wish is my command. Always will be, always was.

Colin brings in the tea on a tray: a cup and saucer, Pasmore's cup, his own

Mrs Pasmore (*to Colin*) He's not like this when you're not here.
Pasmore Nay, when you're not here, Colin I'm on my knees. In adoration. Morning, noon and night. Eight hours of grovelling, eight hours of working, eight hours of sleep.
Mrs Pasmore He doesn't work at all, love. Thank you. (*She takes the cup and saucer after she sits*)
Pasmore I vacuum. I clean. I cut the lawn. I light the fire. I fetch the coal. I drive you to the shops.
Mrs Pasmore He makes it sound like a torment. He's in front of that television from five in the evening till twelve at night, children's programmes, the news, the lot. I don't know where to put myself at times. I get fed up of listening.
Pasmore Watching. Watching. Women: they run this house. When Wendy's here, or Eileen—or Wendy *and* Eileen—I go hide in a cupboard. No sooner show my head than it's fetch this, fetch that. I felt safer down the pit.
Mrs Pasmore You couldn't wait to get out.

Pasmore Now I can't wait to get back in.
Mrs Pasmore Lies. All lies.
Pasmore Don't worry. She can tell a tale or two.
Mrs Pasmore Should hear him over the fence to Mrs Halliday next door. She's twenty-five. You'd think *he* was twenty-seven.
Pasmore The spirit is all that counts.
Mrs Pasmore Leaning on the fence to hold himself up: you'd think he was trying to court her.
Pasmore She knows a good-looker when she sees one.
Mrs Pasmore You're old enough to be her father.
Pasmore It's not age that counts, but spirit.
Colin You were commending the loyalty of marriage, Dad, a while ago.
Pasmore She knows I wouldn't leave her.
Mrs Pasmore (*to Colin*) At his age, love, he wouldn't stand much chance.
Pasmore One foot on that fence, she's off. (*He signals next door*) She takes a joke. Her husband runs a boutique. In town. Gets his trade in summer, and scarcely ought for the rest of the year. He comes home and hangs about the house, a face as long as this. She prefers a bit of a joker.
Mrs Pasmore A joker!
Pasmore (*to Colin*) I tell her one or two tales.
Mrs Pasmore As tall as this house. And always boasts.
Pasmore Something to boast about, my love.
Mrs Pasmore She's heard it all. A thousand times.
Colin You're not quarrelling, are you?
Pasmore This is light conversation, lad. (*He leans across and pats Mrs Pasmore's hand*)
Mrs Pasmore I'm going back to bed. I only got up for a glass of water.
Pasmore You've had a cup of tea.
Mrs Pasmore Colin made it. I wouldn't turn his offer down. Would I, love?
Colin You could have had water, if you'd preferred.
Mrs Pasmore I was glad to take it. (*She rises*) I usually have a cup of water by the bed. I forgot tonight with your coming. Do you want any more blankets, love?
Colin I'm fine.
Mrs Pasmore You'll find them in that cupboard. In the little back room. It's the only time we use upstairs when you, or Wendy or Eileen come.
Pasmore Didn't you take your pills?
Mrs Pasmore I did.
Pasmore (*to Colin*) For arthritis. They make her sleep as well.
Mrs Pasmore It was the cup of water. (*To Colin*) I usually wake up, take a sip, and drop straight off. I won't stay longer.
Colin Goodnight, then, Mother.
Mrs Pasmore Goodnight, then, love.
Colin And congratulations.
Mrs Pasmore Oh, thank you, love. (*She nods to Pasmore*)

Mrs Pasmore goes to her bedroom. The door closes behind her and the chair is knocked again with the walking stick

Pasmore Been through one or two hard times.
Colin You have.
Pasmore Stuck together.
Colin That's right.
Pasmore Thick and thin. Her thick, me thin. (*He laughs, picks up his tea and drinks*) Be getting back myself. Stay down, if you want. There are one or two books to read. Adventure stories. Anything you want?
Colin No thanks.
Pasmore Grand having you home.
Colin Good being back.
Pasmore See you in the morning.
Colin Goodnight, Dad.
Pasmore Goodnight, lad.

Pasmore goes into the passage taking the cup with him. He coughs slightly and opens his bedroom door. He switches the light on

Pasmore enters the bedroom and closes the door. There is a further cough from the other side.

The light goes off in Mrs Pasmore's room. After a moment the light in Pasmore's room goes off too

Colin turns to the fire. He lies back in the chair, watching the fire. He draws his dressing gown further round him. He drinks tea, then puts the cup down. He lies back, his eyes fixed on the fire

The Lights fade to a black-out

SCENE 2

The same. Morning

Light shines through the windows. The sound of the radio from the kitchen. The back door opens

Pasmore comes in with a bucket of coal. He wears trousers, a shirt, a pullover, and slippers

He comes into the living-room and puts the bucket by the fire. He pokes the fire, and straightens up

Mrs Pasmore comes out of her bedroom, wearing a dress and cardigan, and carrying her walking-stick

Mrs Pasmore Colin up?
Pasmore Sleeps theer all day, tha knows.
Mrs Pasmore I don't think so. Not like some.
Pasmore I only slept in after I gev up work. (*He indicates the fire*) Stayed in. Bit o' coal on.

Act I, Scene 2

Mrs Pasmore We ought to order another ton. It's running out in the bunker.
Pasmore I'll do it. Leave it to me.
Mrs Pasmore If I left anything to you it would never be done. Have you had any breakfast?
Pasmore What I want.
Mrs Pasmore I only want a piece of toast. (*She goes into the kitchen*)
Pasmore The kettle's boiled. (*He picks up his cup of tea which is standing, hot, on the mantelpiece*) The piece of toast is already cooked.
Mrs Pasmore How did you know I'd want one? (*She turns the radio off*)
Pasmore Toast is usually on the menu. This morning, I assume, no different from any other.
Mrs Pasmore It's hot.
Pasmore I've just done it. I was going to bring it in, until I heard you moving about. Breakfast in bed.
Mrs Pasmore I never have breakfast in bed. (*She butters the toast*)
Pasmore Today, I thought, is special.
Mrs Pasmore Oh, today.
Pasmore (*calling through*) Many happy anniversaries, love.
Mrs Pasmore Thank you.
Pasmore (*to himself*) She doesn't give a damn. Yes, she does. No, she doesn't. Trying not to show it. (*He pokes the fire again and sits*)
Mrs Pasmore (*coming into the living-room*) Thank you, love. That was very much appreciated. And thank you for sixty years of a very happily married life.
Pasmore Been one or two ups and downs.
Mrs Pasmore No more than most, and fewer than some. (*She kisses him, stooping to his chair*) Thank you, love.

Pasmore is clearly moved

Colin here as well.
Pasmore That's right.
Mrs Pasmore Make a day of it.
Pasmore We can. (*He weeps, without covering, however, or lowering his head*)
Mrs Pasmore I'll just go get my breakfast. (*She returns to the kitchen, puts the piece of toast on a plate and pours a cup of tea from the pot*)

Pasmore sits by the fire, gazing at it. Mrs Pasmore sits composedly in the kitchen, her air—and look—one of abstraction, as she eats her toast, about which she is fastidious; but not overly so

What were you talking about last night?
Pasmore Sebastopol.
Mrs Pasmore You were never there. (*She eats*)
Pasmore Where do you think I got my wound?
Mrs Pasmore I thought it was Constantinople.

Pasmore I was climbing over the wall when the eunuch got me with his sword. (*He bares a leg above his sock to examine the scar*) Would you believe it, after all these years.
Mrs Pasmore You shouldn't have been there.
Pasmore We took the wrong turning. This naval chap told us where to go. Said it was a club.
Mrs Pasmore I suppose it was.
Pasmore His sword wa' like a razor. I've never jumped higher either afore or since.
Mrs Pasmore What's that got to do with Sebastopol?
Pasmore I was in the Crimea before Constantinople.
Mrs Pasmore Of course you were.
Pasmore You get dozier every minute.
Mrs Pasmore So do you.
Pasmore I've some excuse.
Mrs Pasmore What excuse? And how can you hold a conversation when you're sitting in the other room?
Pasmore I'm not holding a conversation. I'm sitting here and supping tea.
Mrs Pasmore You're talking to me.
Pasmore I was answering a question. Do you want me to get up every time you talk?
Mrs Pasmore Why have you some excuse?
Pasmore To do what?
Mrs Pasmore *To get dozier.*
Pasmore I've lost half me lungs with pneumoconiosis. I've no circulation, and me heart's a quarter of the strength it should be.
Mrs Pasmore Who told you that?
Pasmore The doctor.
Mrs Pasmore He never told me.
Pasmore It wasn't you he was examining.
Mrs Pasmore He usually tells me when you go to see him.
Pasmore This is the Pensions Board. When I asked for compensation.
Mrs Pasmore Oh, then.
Pasmore If it wa're a quarter fifteen year ago it must be nearer a sixteenth by now.
Mrs Pasmore I've told you to watch it when you're carrying coal.
Pasmore I do watch it. God damn it.
Mrs Pasmore You'll be waking Colin, shouting through.

Pasmore slams the arm of his chair, but doesn't answer. He lifts his cup of tea to drink but doesn't bother; he puts it back down

What did you tell him about Sebastopol?
Pasmore I told him we'd marched to Rostov-on-Don.
Mrs Pasmore I thought you went to save the Tsar.
Pasmore The Tsar was shot. (*Pause*) I told him how we'd marched all the way back again.
Mrs Pasmore To Sebastopol.
Pasmore Fighting women.

Act I, Scene 2

Mrs Pasmore Women?
Pasmore Every step.
Mrs Pasmore Why women?
Pasmore Because they're all smiling and cooing and covering it up, but hell's own bloody demons underneath.
Mrs Pasmore There's no need to swear.
Pasmore I wasn't swearing.
Mrs Pasmore I distinctly heard you swear. On Sunday morning.
Pasmore It isn't Sunday morning.
Mrs Pasmore What is it?
Pasmore God knows. (*He picks up the paper and tries to read without his glasses; he can't, so he puts it down*) It's not Sunday.
Mrs Pasmore Every day is alike up here.
Pasmore Except Sunday.

Mrs Pasmore finishes her breakfast and dusts her hands of toast

Mrs Pasmore What's so different then?
Pasmore No milkman.
Mrs Pasmore I never hear him, in any case.

Mrs Pasmore clears up, briefly, before bringing a fresh cup of tea through

(*Calling*) Do you want another pot?
Pasmore No, thank you.
Mrs Pasmore I can bring you one.
Pasmore I said no thanks.
Mrs Pasmore If that's what you want.
Pasmore (*to himself*) If I did want one I should have said I did.
Mrs Pasmore (*entering*) What's that?
Pasmore I said it's cold.
Mrs Pasmore It shouldn't be with that fire. (*She sits, after setting the cup on the coffee table*) I thought Colin might be.
Pasmore I don't think he will.
Mrs Pasmore I think he might.

She gets up, with great difficulty and moves her chair fractionally to a better position. She adjusts the coffee table, and sits again

Well, then ... (*She sips the tea; puts it down. Pause*) Have you heard the news?
Pasmore You turned it off.
Mrs Pasmore I turned it off because no one was listening.
Pasmore I was listening.
Mrs Pasmore I didn't see you.
Pasmore You don't have to see in order to listen.
Mrs Pasmore Don't you. (*Complacently, she sips tea*)
Pasmore Listened to it for long enough.
Mrs Pasmore We have.
Pasmore How many years?
Mrs Pasmore Too many.

Pasmore I thought you welcomed every year.
Mrs Pasmore I was married.
Pasmore You are married.
Mrs Pasmore To you.
Pasmore I know you're married to me.
Mrs Pasmore Oh, what's the use? Born stupid, stay stupid.
Pasmore You're referring to the chap next door.
Mrs Pasmore I'm referring to you. (*She picks up the newspaper*)
Pasmore That's yesterday's paper.
Mrs Pasmore As a matter of fact (*she examines the top of the page*) it's the day before's.
Pasmore If you hadn't have turned off the radio we'd have heard today's.
Mrs Pasmore You'll hear it again this evening.
Pasmore Might not be here this evening.
Mrs Pasmore Going somewhere, are you?
Pasmore Might not be here. Full stop.
Mrs Pasmore You've been threatening to die for twenty-five years.
Pasmore So have you.
Mrs Pasmore I had a hysterectomy.
Pasmore I had pneumoconiosis. (*He coughs*) Gets no better. Your condition gets no worse.
Mrs Pasmore I have other ailments.
Pasmore Such as?
Mrs Pasmore Never you mind. (*She reads with no great attention, the newspaper raised above the level of her eyes*)
Pasmore Might be something contagious. If it is, I ought to know.
Mrs Pasmore If it's infectious.
Pasmore Is it infectious? You never said.
Mrs Pasmore I said if it's infectious you ought to know. Since it isn't you can set your mind at rest.
Pasmore What is it?
Mrs Pasmore You know well enough.
Pasmore If I know well enough would I trouble to ask?
Mrs Pasmore Pity people who retire couldn't stay in work. (*She is absorbed in the newspaper*)
Pasmore I couldn't do a day's work to save my life.
Mrs Pasmore Don't I know.
Pasmore You've nothing to complain of. No, she hasn't. Not a thing. I worked long enough to keep her going. Yes, I did.
Mrs Pasmore I'm appreciative of it. Don't you worry. You don't have to fret.
Pasmore Might show it, in that case, from time to time.
Mrs Pasmore I do show it.

The back door opens. Wendy comes in. She is slightly built, an attractive woman, in her mid-forties, well-preserved and well-dressed. She carries a bunch of flowers

Mrs Pasmore puts the paper down and half-turns, after listening

That's not Colin? (*She half-rises*) He must have gone out. (*She gets up*)
Pasmore I'd have heard him if he had.
Mrs Pasmore (*calling*) Colin?

Wendy quietly closes the back door, aware of their voices

Did you leave the door unfastened?
Pasmore I fetched a bucket of coal this morning. (*He rises and goes to the living-room door as Wendy takes off her coat*) Colin?

They meet in the kitchen

Wendy Hello, Father.
Pasmore Good God.
Wendy (*kissing him*) Happy anniversary, love! (*She hands him the flowers*)
Pasmore What are you doing here?
Wendy I've come to see you!
Pasmore Better give these to your mother.
Mrs Pasmore (*crossing the room*) Wendy, love!
Wendy (*entering*) Happy anniversary, Mother.
Mrs Pasmore Thank you. Thank you, love (*She takes the flowers*)

Wendy embraces her

Wendy How are you?
Mrs Pasmore I'm well. What a surprise. Colin yesterday. Now this.

Pasmore comes into the room

Wendy What a welcome! (*She indicates Pasmore*) "What are you doing here?"
Pasmore The shock. The shock.
Wendy Give us a kiss!

She embraces Pasmore, who kisses her cheek. Immediately, on being released, Pasmore coughs

Choking to death, then, are you?
Pasmore I'm off cigarettes. No more smoking for me.
Wendy Better put these in water. (*She takes the flowers from Mrs Pasmore*) Is there a vase in the kitchen? (*She goes to the kitchen*)
Mrs Pasmore In the cupboard, love.
Pasmore Cupboard love. (*He indicates the newspaper*)
Mrs Pasmore Eight letters. "Stored affection." (*She picks up the newspaper which is folded back to the crossword*) Cupboard. (*She puts down the paper and looks round for a pencil*)
Pasmore (*calling*) Are you staying?
Wendy Of course I'm staying.
Pasmore I wondered.
Wendy Wonder no more. (*She gets a vase from the kitchen cupboard*)
Pasmore Do you want a cup of tea?
Wendy You both sit down. I'll do it. (*Having got the vase, she arranges the flowers in it, then makes herself a cup of tea*)

Mrs Pasmore C.U.P.B. ...
Pasmore O.R.
Mrs Pasmore (*writing, then*) It's not B.O.R.
Pasmore B.O.R.E.
Mrs Pasmore It's B.O.*A*.R.D.
Pasmore (*calling through*) How do you spell cupboard?
Wendy C.U.P. ...
Mrs Pasmore (*calling through*) B.O.A.R.D.
Wendy Correct.
Mrs Pasmore Eight letters.
Pasmore I'm ignorant. (*He sits back down*) I'm only good for shifting muck.
Mrs Pasmore You are. (*She prints letters in the paper*) Where it has P it should have W.
Pasmore You've got it wrong.
Mrs Pasmore It's you who said cupboard.
Pasmore I said cupboard love.
Mrs Pasmore The third letter should be W.
Pasmore Cowboard.
Mrs Pasmore You see. I've got it wrong. Following your instructions.
Pasmore (*calling*) Have you driven over, Wendy?
Wendy Two hours.
Pasmore Shouldn't take as long as that.
Wendy Rush-hour coming through the towns.
Pasmore Do you want a hand?
Wendy Sit yourself down.
Pasmore Cowboard.
Mrs Pasmore (*putting paper and pencil down*) When I met you, you were ridiculous. You're still ridiculous now.

Wendy enters with the flowers

(*To Wendy*) There! They look lovely, love.
Pasmore Grand!
Mrs Pasmore Beautiful.
Wendy (*setting the vase down*) Sure you don't want another cup?
Pasmore No, thank you.
Mrs Pasmore It was me she was asking.
Pasmore Me an' all.
Wendy Both of you shut up! (*She goes out to the kitchen*) I'll throw the teapot over you.
Mrs Pasmore You've upset her.
Pasmore It's you's upset her.
Mrs Pasmore It was you.
Pasmore I said nowt.
Mrs Pasmore It's you that keeps interfering.
Pasmore I offered you a clue.
Mrs Pasmore Shut up!

Pause

Act I, Scene 2

Wendy comes in with her tea. She looks at both of them, chooses a chair and sits

Pause

Wendy That's Colin's car outside.
Pasmore He came last night.
Wendy Why didn't you tell me?
Pasmore You never asked.
Mrs Pasmore I mentioned it, Wendy. In the rush you never heard.
Pasmore You get your temper from her, tha knows.
Wendy I get it from both of you, if the truth were known.
Pasmore I'm as good as gold. I've nowt to complain at. It's she who's allus on a high horse.
Mrs Pasmore High horse!
Pasmore Low horse, then.
Mrs Pasmore (*to Wendy*) Isn't he ridiculous?
Wendy I've driven seventy miles and all you do is bicker.
Mrs Pasmore I'm not bickering: it's him.
Pasmore It's her.
Mrs Pasmore It's him ...

Pause

Wendy There we are, then. (*She sips her tea*)
Pasmore Would you like a biscuit?
Wendy No thank you, Dad. Do you want one, Mother?
Mrs Pasmore No thank you, love.
Wendy Still in bed? (*She gestures*) Colin.
Mrs Pasmore He was down here half the night.
Pasmore Closer to a quarter.
Mrs Pasmore I'd say half ...
Wendy How's Kay and the children?

Pause

Mrs Pasmore They're fine.
Pasmore They're grand.
Mrs Pasmore How's Arnold?
Wendy I haven't seen him for the past two months.
Pasmore You're not divorced already?
Wendy Not quite.
Pasmore I don't know why you bother.
Wendy Why not?
Pasmore Nay, you've lived with him for twenty-odd year: if you didn't know what he wa' like till now you mustn't have had your head screwed on. (*To Mrs Pasmore*) It's ever since she started with all these bloody politics.
Wendy What politics?
Pasmore Labour Party. God Christ. A set o' Mary Ellens.
Wendy I'm not with the Party any more.

Pasmore What are you?
Wendy I'm Independent.
Pasmore You can bloody well say that again.
Mrs Pasmore Have you gone Independent, love?
Wendy Don't make it sound like an infectious disease.
Pasmore Contagious. We have that in this house.

A bang overhead

    Colin.
Mrs Pasmore I'm not surprised. The noise you make.
Pasmore It's thy daughter does the shouting.
Mrs Pasmore It's your daughter as well.
Pasmore Nay, the milkman wa' round a lot the year that she wa' born. And the postman. Not to mention the rentman. "Rent and rates!" he'd call at the door, coming in, tha knows, wi'out knocking.
Mrs Pasmore What a thing to say to your daughter!
Pasmore You can say ought you like to her. Can't you, love? She's a politician. You're not crying, are you?
Wendy I'm blowing my nose.
Mrs Pasmore You were always harder on the girls than you were on Colin.
Wendy He was harder on Colin, I always thought.
Pasmore Theer, then. I wa're hard on no one.

Pause

Wendy blows her nose and puts her handkerchief away

Wendy Sixty years!
Pasmore Sixty years o' penal servitude. (*He looks into the cup and drinks*)
Mrs Pasmore He's showing off to his daughter.
Pasmore I'm not showing off.
Mrs Pasmore You are.
Pasmore I'm not.
Mrs Pasmore I say you are.

Pause

Pasmore I said ... (*Pause*) If she's been married all these years—in sickness and in health—she might have hung on a little longer.
Wendy I have hung on a little longer.
Pasmore A little longer still.
Wendy Until I die!
Pasmore We're hanging on until we die.
Mrs Pasmore We're not hanging on at all.
Pasmore We're not hanging on at all.
Mrs Pasmore That's right.
Pasmore We accepted each other for what we are.
Mrs Pasmore We did.
Pasmore I'm not sure what that is. But whatever it was—I accepted it.
Mrs Pasmore You're like two peas in a pod.

Wendy Me and Arnold?
Mrs Pasmore You and your father.
Pasmore I allus thought she wa' more like you. *Colin*, I thought, is more like me. Quiet and thoughtful.

Wendy laughs

Mrs Pasmore I'm saying nothing.
Pasmore (*to Wendy*) Saint Hilda. (*He indicates Mrs Pasmore*)

Wendy laughs again. She drinks her tea, looks round, puts the cup down

Mrs Pasmore Why should she make the rest of her life a misery if, by getting divorced, she can improve it?
Pasmore She wept buckets when she first found out. "Wendy," she said. "And *Arnold*." You should have seen her.
Mrs Pasmore In principle I'm against it. In practice, though, I'm not.
Pasmore She'll be asking me to divorce her next.
Mrs Pasmore It's not too late.
Pasmore After sixty years.
Mrs Pasmore It's not too long.
Pasmore (*to Wendy*) In addition to which you were married in church.
Wendy What's that got to do with it?
Pasmore Your vows. Made before God. When you get up there you'll have a lot of bloody explaining to do.
Wendy I got married in church because of you.
Pasmore Me?
Wendy And my mother.
Mrs Pasmore *Me?*
Wendy And Arnold.
Pasmore He'd never been inside a church.
Wendy You said it didn't matter.
Pasmore Nay, I've said enough. Here's Colin.

Colin comes down the stairs. He is dressed in trousers, a pullover and an open-necked shirt

Wendy rises

Colin goes to the kitchen with the cup he's brought down. He rinses it out. He puts the kettle on. He sees Wendy's coat flung over the stool, picks it up, puts it down, and goes through to the living-room, opening the door

Colin Wendy!
Wendy Our kid! (*She embraces him*)
Colin It's good to see you.
Wendy (*holding him at arm's length*) London not doing you much harm.
Colin It's had long enough to try.
Wendy How's the family?
Colin Not bad. How's yours?
Wendy Divorced. Or will be in a couple of months.
Colin Glad about it?

Wendy Not half!
Pasmore Don't mind us. We're not here. (*To Colin*) Do you want a pot of tea?
Colin I've put it on.
Pasmore I'll mek it. Story of my life. Do this. Do that. Do t'other.
Mrs Pasmore It's a wonder he does anything at all, the advertising that goes on before he starts.
Pasmore (*to Colin*) Sit down. It's done. (*He goes to the kitchen leaving the door open*)
Colin You should have said you were coming.
Wendy I didn't know until I'd left.
Colin How're you going to make a living without your husband?
Pasmore (*calling*) She's got a job. She'll earn more inside six months in attendance money as a local councillor than you can earn in over a year.
Wendy That's why I'm getting divorced. Give more time to the job.
Pasmore (*calling through*) She's gone Independent.
Wendy I *am* independent. I haven't gone.
Mrs Pasmore That's always been her motto.
Pasmore (*calling*) Husband a company director; wife a working-class representative. It always did look bloody silly.
Wendy "It's either the Party or your husband," they said. I decided to give up both.
Pasmore (*calling*) Your sister's sold out. Sold out on *us*. I wa' down the pit for forty-five years.
Wendy (*calling back*) You voted Conservative at the last election.
Pasmore (*calling*) I did not. (*He comes to the room door*) Your mother voted Conservative.
Mrs Pasmore I wanted someone in charge who knew what they were doing. After fifty years of waffling I wanted to see someone in charge who believed in what they said, said it without equivocation, and went and did it. What's the word? (*She picks up the newspaper*)
Pasmore Nine across. Four letters.
Mrs Pasmore (*finds it*) Cant! Sixty years as a collier's wife. It sums it up exactly.
Wendy Stabbed in the back by my mother.
Pasmore They're all Conservative round here. Boarding-house owners, shopkeepers. Farmers. Businesses. You couldn't raise a Labour vote round here if you looked from now till Christmas.
Mrs Pasmore Socialism's worn out. We voted for it, in power and out, for fifty-five years. Where's it got us? It isn't socialism that gives you better conditions. It's whether the country wants to work or not. Like Germany. Or France. Or Japan. They've leapt ahead and we, with labour disputes and demarcations—politicized trade unions: I've heard it from him (*she indicates Pasmore*)—are one of the poorest industrialized countries in Europe.
Pasmore Ay up! Kettle! (*He goes*)
Wendy I never knew you were so militant, love.

Act I, Scene 2

Mrs Pasmore It makes you sick. Night after night. Watching that. (*She indicates the television*) *Asking* for jobs. "If I haven't got a job someone's got to give me one!" There's never been such a gutless generation.
Wendy An evangelist! My God.
Mrs Pasmore I won't have His name profaned. Not in this house. You can profane God's name outside, but not in here.
Wendy You can see what affluence has done for them.
Colin Nay, don't blame me.
Mrs Pasmore Colin has done very well. He didn't sit on his bottom and say, "I want! I want!" he got up and created ... what did you create? My mind's confused at the moment.
Wendy *The Last Evangelist*, Mother.
Mrs Pasmore He wrote a book called *The Last Evangelist*, the money from which he sensibly invested.
Wendy Buying, amongst other things, a bungalow for you.
Mrs Pasmore Taking the burden off the community.
Wendy We could do with you on our Council, Mother.
Mrs Pasmore Don't worry. Your father and I have lived through harder times than this. (*She indicates the television*) It makes me weep to see well-fed, well-clad people, with subsidized housing and a National Health, with state benefits and pensions, complaining they've never had a chance. If their muscles were exercised as much as their mouths they'd have created ten thousand jobs apiece.
Pasmore (*coming in with Colin's tea and a cup of his own*) Five across. Six letters.
Mrs Pasmore It's seven letters as a matter of fact. (*She consults the newspaper again*)
Pasmore "Needless complaining."
Mrs Pasmore *Whining*.
Pasmore She gets all the words from that.
Mrs Pasmore Not quite.
Pasmore And all her ideas from the television. I'm ashamed to go out with her at times. A well-known socialist all my life and she'd make Mussolini look like the local vicar.
Mrs Pasmore How many union meetings have you come home from saying unions and politics shouldn't mix: the one holds back the other?
Pasmore I said the other holds back the one. (*He laughs, sitting down*)
Mrs Pasmore "Workers, shirkers": that's what people are chanting now. It makes me ashamed to have been one.
Pasmore You never were.
Mrs Pasmore I brought up three children! On wages that would be a pittance to the unemployed today. I hadn't a halfpenny in the house from Tuesday night till Friday lunch-time. No gas when we ran out of pennies. Pennies! Nowadays, if the gas is cut off they get a grant to put it back on.
Wendy What did she have for supper, love?
Pasmore Nay, all I do is bloody work. She has the ideas. A woman's world. It allus was.
Mrs Pasmore That's right.

Pasmore Work down a coalmine, eight hours a day—day or night, as near as not—while she's up top, having ideas.
Mrs Pasmore If someone came complaining to me about what they can get for sitting on their bottom I'd give them a kick right up it. "I haven't had this. I haven't had that." I'd show them what they could have. There'd be no unemployment by the time I'd finished.
Wendy No wonder she voted Tory.
Mrs Pasmore I voted for common sense.
Wendy What're you doing for lunch?
Pasmore Lunch?
Wendy We'll take you out. (*She indicates Colin*) Have a spin along the front.
Mrs Pasmore I ought to choose some clothes. I'm not sure I've anything to go out in.
Pasmore She's tons of clothes in theer.
Mrs Pasmore I've one wardrobe. One cupboard. One set of drawers.
Pasmore I've two pair of trousers. Two jackets. One suit. Two pairs of shoes.
Mrs Pasmore By choice. (*She looks at him*)
Pasmore Her choice. (*He sees her look*) Nay, I can only wear one pair of trousers and one jacket at a time. If one of them conks out I only need one other.
Wendy We can go for a drive in the country, come back over the moors and have lunch at that hotel.
Pasmore The Waldorf.
Wendy The Waldorf! What do you think, our kid?
Colin Fine.
Mrs Pasmore (*getting up; to Wendy*) I'm that pleased you've come over, love. I want to find something special. (*She moves to her room*)
Pasmore I'd better look, an' all. I'll look at one shoe, then I'll look at the other. I'll look at the one coat, then I'll look at its mate. I'll look at one pair of trousers . . .

Mrs Pasmore disappears into her room, closing the door

Pasmore looks from Colin to Wendy and back again

I shan't be a minute. (*He winks from the door*)

Pasmore goes to his room and closes the door

Pause

Wendy (*sitting companionably beside Colin*) What you been up to?
Colin A history of New York.
Wendy New York!
Colin Purely as a hobby. I went there with the book. In a curious way it seemed like home.
Wendy Home.

Act I, Scene 2   21

Colin The same provincial squalor. The same curious lack of guile. I've never met such an open-hearted people. Everything there is tenuous, despite its air of permanance and size ... otherwise I'm back at college.
Wendy Charles the Second.
Colin Right.
Wendy "The thought of England surges up before me. I am recalling what is for me the most important historical period of all, the reign of the Puritans and Oliver Cromwell."
Colin Freud, in a letter to his wife, on his coming to exile in England.
Wendy I began to think it was you, you quoted it so often, Colin.
Colin Aye! (*He laughs*) I haven't changed, our kid.
Wendy Still out to impress.
Colin That's right.
Wendy What drew you to The Evangelist?
Colin You're right. Not my period at all.
Wendy Eighteen oh-eight to eighteen forty-seven.
Colin Remember the dates?
Wendy I read the book!
Colin One summer vacation I was home from college, I was reading in the local library and came across *The Prophecies of Jonathan Wroe*. There I was, sitting at the edge of our parents' housing estate which stretched across a one-time moor where, one hundred and twenty years before, an impoverished youth, who worked in a local mill, had visions, or so he said, of heaven and hell. I looked up newspapers of that time and came across accounts of his last crusade: blowing up bridges, setting fire to mills, de-railing trains—battles in the Pennine hills, with the local militia then with troops sent up from London. It came alive in a way that no other period ever could. It seemed remarkable that a product of the Industrial Revolution could see the consequences so far ahead, the despoilation, the conformity, the dilution of feeling—the de-spiritualization, as our mother, if she ever found it in her crossword, might describe it—which have turned us into the people we are today.
Wendy I never understood why he gave himself up.
Colin His father died when he was twelve. He became the sole provider for a family of seven. Was he, he asked himself, his mother's son, or was he his mother's husband? At the height of his campaign his mother was arrested. On the authorities' promise to release her he gave himself up. One day, in the City Museum, I came across a print: it showed a barrack-like square, the anonymous windows of a plain stone building, a line of red-clad soldiers, a scaffold, and two trussed figures: to add significance to their execution, they were hanged successively, the mother before the son, a few feet apart, and face to face. A short while later I stepped out into a cobbled yard not unlike the one in the print itself and decided that day to write the book.

Pause

Pasmore emerges from his bedroom carrying a dark suit on a hanger. He carries it down the passage to the back door

Pasmore (*as he passes Mrs Pasmore's door*) Moth balls.

Mrs Pasmore's door immediately opens

Mrs Pasmore (*calling*) He's kept it in that cupboard so long it must be smelling musty.
Pasmore (*at the back door*) I've had no need to put it on.

He exits, closing the back door behind him

Mrs Pasmore We used to have moth balls. That was years ago. I shan't be a minute.
Wendy You're not changing already?
Mrs Pasmore Not yet. (*She closes the door*)
Wendy Cant!
Colin *Cant!*

They laugh

There is a tapping on the front door

Wendy rises

Wendy (*calling*) I'll get it.
Colin You sit down.

Colin goes out to the passage. He disappears towards the front door

Wendy, having risen, glances about the room. There is the sound of bolts being drawn, a key turned, a chain released

Wendy picks up Mrs Pasmore's folded newspaper

Wendy (*reading*) "Needless complaining."
Colin (*off*) Eileen!
Eileen (*off*) What on earth are you doing here?
Colin (*off*) Come in!
Eileen (*off*) I am in.

Eileen appears in the passageway. She is well-built, middle fifties in appearance, though older. Robust; modestly dressed in a heavy coat and scarf

Eileen (*off*) How long have you been up?
Colin (*off*) I came last night.
Eileen (*at the room door*) I don't believe it!
Wendy Great minds!
Eileen *Great minds.*

Wendy and Eileen embrace

Pasmore enters the kitchen

When did you get here?
Wendy An hour ago.

Act I, Scene 2   23

Eileen Must have passed me on the road. There's something the matter with the engine. (*She draws off her gloves*)
Wendy Engine?
Eileen The car's that slow.
Wendy We could have come together.
Eileen Ridiculous. Both live in the same town. Last time I mentioned it you said you wouldn't be able.
Wendy I found I could.

Colin takes Eileen's coat

Eileen And Colin. (*To Colin*) Thank you, love.
Wendy Jack come with you?
Eileen Teaching.

Pasmore, having delayed himself at the sound of her voice, putting the kettle on in the kitchen, appears at the living-room door

Pasmore It's you.
Eileen How are you, Father? (*She embraces Pasmore*)
Pasmore All right. (*He receives Eileen's embrace*)
Eileen Sulking, are you?
Pasmore Suit's on the clothes-line. Full o' moth-balls.
Wendy It's not.
Pasmore It's full o' summat.
Wendy It's full of not being used.
Eileen Congratulations (*She kisses his cheek*)
Pasmore What on?
Eileen We're not going to have to chase you with a stick? That's what he used to do with us. You are going to cheer up, Father.
Pasmore I am cheered up.
Wendy He was as bright as a penny until you arrived.
Pasmore I should have had warning. My constitution's not used to all this noise.

Mrs Pasmore comes out of her room having changed

Mrs Pasmore Is that our Eileen?
Eileen It is, Mother!
Mrs Pasmore (*entering the living room*) How are you, love?
Eileen Lovely to see you.

Eileen and Mrs Pasmore embrace warmly

Pasmore I thought we weren't going for another two hours. My suit's on the clothes-line. It'll be hours afore I'm ready.
Mrs Pasmore We can go whenever you like. (*To Eileen*) I thought I'd change. I'm so fed up of the same old clothes.
Eileen Congratulations, love (*She embraces her mother again*)
Pasmore Keep your voice down.
Mrs Pasmore Whatever for?

Pasmore Round here it's considered unnatural to be wed for more'n a year. Nob'dy'll bloody believe it.

A bang at the front door

What did I tell you?
Colin I'll get it. (*He goes to the front door*)
Pasmore It can't be another. We only had three kiddies.
Mrs Pasmore (*to Eileen*) Do you want a cup of tea?
Eileen I'd love one.
Pasmore (*going*) I'll get it. The kettle's on. (*He goes to the kitchen*)
Eileen Anybody'd think he wasn't glad to see you.
Mrs Pasmore That's the way he shows it, love. (*She raises her voice*) That's the way he covers it up.
Pasmore (*calling*) In this house there's bloody well nowt to cover.
Mrs Pasmore And don't swear.
Pasmore (*calling*) I'm not swearing.
Mrs Pasmore I say you are.
Pasmore (*calling*) I'm expressing an opinion. (*He makes tea in the kitchen*)
Colin (*entering*) Post. (*He hands some envelopes to Mrs Pasmore*)
Wendy Two telegrams.
Mrs Pasmore (*calling*) Tommy!
Pasmore (*calling*) I can't mek it any faster. God damn and blast.
Wendy Come and read your post.

Wendy ushers him into the room as she goes out to the kitchen

Pasmore What post?
Wendy Come and read it.
Pasmore Thy husband not with you?
Eileen Jack's in school, Dad. He sends you both his love.
Pasmore Where is it? (*He looks round*)
Eileen Give us a hug. (*She hugs him, bear-like, to her*)
Pasmore She's going to crush me to bloody death. How Jack's put up with it all these years I can't mek out. No wonder he's the size he is.
Eileen He's very well.
Pasmore He's very thin.
Eileen He's very slender.
Pasmore He doesn't weigh more than two or three pounds.
Eileen I'll give you a thick ear, if you don't watch out.
Mrs Pasmore Give over bickering and look at this. (*Having opened the first envelope, she has removed a card, read its message with great care, and now hands it to Pasmore*)
Pasmore I can't see without my glasses. (*He screws up his eyes to read*)
Mrs Pasmore You can see well enough.
Pasmore From Colin's children.
Mrs Pasmore All four of them have clubbed together.
Pasmore It doesn't take much clubbing together to buy a card. What's this squiggle?

Act I, Scene 2

Mrs Pasmore That's Susan.
Pasmore Education: since these lot went to school, it's gone to the dogs. (*He reads*) "Congratulations Grandma and Grandpa." Signed Susan, Cynthia, Kenneth and Paul. That's very nice. Thank you, Colin.
Mrs Pasmore Thank you, love.
Colin It'll be Susan. She usually initiates these things.
Mrs Pasmore This is one of Eileen's. (*She hands a card to Pasmore*) Thank you, love.
Pasmore Aye, thank you, love.
Mrs Pasmore I always recognize Eric's writing. He writes to us a lot.
Eileen What about your telegrams?
Mrs Pasmore I'll get to those, don't worry.

Wendy brings in Eileen's tea

Wendy Sugar?
Eileen One, love.

Wendy holds the bowl; Eileen takes sugar

Colin I'll take it. (*He takes the sugar back to the kitchen*) Anyone else want tea?
Wendy No thank you.
Mrs Pasmore (*reading a card*) No thank you, love.
Pasmore (*shaking his head*) No thanks.

Colin puts the sugar bowl down in the kitchen. He sits on a stool and gazes out of the back window

Mrs Pasmore (*reading*) "From Eric and Patrick." Thank you, Eileen. (*She kisses her cheek*) They're both grand childen, love.
Pasmore I know they're both grandchildren.
Mrs Pasmore (*to Eileen*) *Grand* grandchildren, love. (*She tears open a telegram*) Well, then. (*She reads it*) That's very nice.
Pasmore Won the pools, then, have we?
Mrs Pasmore It's from Arnold.
Wendy Arnold!
Mrs Pasmore It's very thoughtful of him.
Pasmore What's he want?
Mrs Pasmore To congratulate us, Tommy. "On your diamond jubilee."
Pasmore Diamond. That's why I'm keeping quiet. I couldn't afford a bit o' glass.

Colin gets up and goes out into the garden through the back door

Mrs Pasmore (*to Wendy*) That's very thoughtful of him, love.
Pasmore Even though we aren't related.
Wendy You will be for another month.
Pasmore In that road, mek best on it we can.
Wendy He's still very fond of you, I know.
Pasmore Is he getting married again?
Wendy We're not even divorced yet, Dad.

Pasmore (*to Eileen*) Grab 'o'd of a woman one day, and grab 'o'd of another the next.
Mrs Pasmore I wish you'd moderate your language.
Pasmore "Four across. Three letter word denoting modern marriage."
Mrs Pasmore This is from you, love.
Pasmore Bed.
Mrs Pasmore (*to Eileen, having opened the second telegram*) "All our love and best wishes. Eileen and Jack." Thank you, love.
Eileen Not at all, Mum. (*They embrace*)
Mrs Pasmore I've always hated "Mum".
Eileen That's what I call Jack's mother. (*To Pasmore*) She can't stand "Mother".
Pasmore My mother I called "Mam".
Mrs Pasmore It always sounded common.
Pasmore She was a wonderful woman.
Mrs Pasmore She couldn't control her children.
Pasmore It was my father who didn't have much control.
Mrs Pasmore She had control over your discipline, but not your education.
Pasmore I left school at eleven.
Mrs Pasmore You were twelve.
Pasmore I was expelled at twelve. I left at eleven.
Wendy What were you expelled for, Dad?
Pasmore For never bloody well being there.
Eileen Where were you?
Pasmore Wukking! What some people nowadays have never heard of. Twelve-hour day, six days a week. Seven miles walk at four in the morning: seven mile back at night. I went to sleep with my clothes on.
Eileen I don't believe it.
Pasmore In a cupboard.
Eileen Rubbish.
Pasmore On a shelf. Out of a family of twelve sons and three daughters, I'm the on'y one still living.
Mrs Pasmore (*handing him the second telegram*) That's Eileen's and Jack's.
Pasmore Didn't need to come as well. Could have saved a couple of bob.
Eileen Do you want me to go back home again?
Mrs Pasmore He doesn't, love.
Wendy Where's Colin?
Eileen He took that sugar out.
Wendy Colin?

Wendy goes out to the kitchen, sees the back door open and goes out

Pasmore I'd better go and get changed, if we're off for a drive.
Eileen Are we going out?
Mrs Pasmore We've planned to, love.
Pasmore We can go in Colin's car.
Eileen Mine almost came to a stop.
Pasmore Summat i' the carburettor. I'll have a look afore you leave.

Act I, Scene 2

Mrs Pasmore He mended our car last week. We had to ask a mechanic to come and get the blessed thing re-started.
Pasmore I'd forgotten a nut. You'd think I'd forgotten a bloody wheel.
Mrs Pasmore It wouldn't go.
Pasmore You could sit in it, couldn't you?
Mrs Pasmore In the garage?
Pasmore I don't know what she wants.
Mrs Pasmore I don't know whether it's old age or he simply puts it on.
Pasmore She lived in a henhouse once.
Mrs Pasmore I did not.
Pasmore Her father was out of work.
Mrs Pasmore He never lived in a henhouse.
Pasmore Talk about meking jobs. All her father made were bloody complaints.
Mrs Pasmore He was wounded in the war! (*To Eileen*) The Boer War, love. It affected the use of his lungs. He worked as hard as any man. He kept being dismissed. They didn't think he worked hard enough. (*She gets a handkerchief from her sleeve and wipes her eyes*) He never explained he was wounded.
Pasmore You did.
Mrs Pasmore I went to his employer. I said, "Do you know you have put a man out of work who gave his health for his country?"
Eileen What did he do?
Mrs Pasmore He laughed in my face.
Pasmore Ask her what she did.
Eileen What did you do, Mother?
Mrs Pasmore (*pause*) I picked up a teapot standing on his desk and emptied it into his lap.
Pasmore He shot out of his bloody chair! Wouldn't strike a woman. Not in those days. Wi' equality, nowadays, o' course, he'd have knocked her around all day.
Mrs Pasmore We never lived in a hen-coop.
Pasmore It had been a hen-coop.
Mrs Pasmore A shed. We were only there seven days.
Pasmore After that, the doss-house.
Mrs Pasmore The People's Home.
Pasmore Used to be called the workhouse.
Mrs Pasmore (*weeping*) A man who had given his health for his country and he was condemned to take his wife and children to the People's Home.
Pasmore The dregs of the earth is that place.
Mrs Pasmore You see how far I've come. All this, from where we started.
Pasmore All my generation, tha knows, are dead. Most of them within eighteen months of retiring. Pneumoconiosis, heart disease, silicosis. I'm the only one left from a generation of colliers that went down the pit just after the First World War. A whole generation: gone.
Mrs Pasmore But for you.
Pasmore And my wife.

Pause. Wendy comes in the back door, followed by Colin who is carrying Pasmore's suit

Wendy (*in a lowered voice*) Are you all right?
Colin Fine.
Wendy You sure?
Colin I'd better take this in. (*He indicates she should go before him*)
Mrs Pasmore Are you going to get ready?
Pasmore I'm off. Shan't take more than two minutes.
Colin (*entering the living room*) Spot of rain. (*He sniffs the suit*) Seems all right.
Pasmore How do you mean, seems? Good bit o' cloth is that. On'y been in it twice. Both times to local funerals.
Mrs Pasmore He has not.
Pasmore His next door but one's. Hers across the road.
Mrs Pasmore (*after a pause*) That's right.
Pasmore In principle I'm allus wrong. Three across: "Put-upon-man. Seven letters."
Eileen Husband!
Pasmore Right.

Pasmore goes, taking the suit, and closes his bedroom door

Mrs Pasmore (*to Eileen*) I'll go and finish, love. Thank you for your cards. Would you put them out? I shan't be long.

Mrs Pasmore goes to her room and closes the door

Eileen begins to lay out the cards and telegrams. Wendy adjusts them on the mantelshelf

Colin Remember when he got a septic thigh? A cut that became infected. In the hospital they said they'd have to cut his leg off. One last chance they said was to put on boiling fomentations. I'd just left him, after a visit. I heard him scream. I went back to the door. Two nurses were holding him down. When two of the other nurses came past, one of them said, "I don't think a human being can stand it. Boiling water, every two hours." At school, I'd gaze out at the hospital across the road. "If he can suffer like that," I thought, "I have to work much harder."
Eileen I remember him going to work with ulcers on his legs.
Wendy He treated them with onions.
Eileen The smell!
Wendy And covered them with a piece of oil-cloth that smelt even more than they did.
Eileen In the bus he used to stand at the back holding onto the seats. When the conductor asked him to sit, he said he couldn't.
Wendy It was true.
Eileen When he came home from work, his legs were covered in pus. He used to sit, groaning, while my mother fed him in the bath.
Wendy The stench.
Eileen How the hell did he stay alive?

Act I, Scene 2

Wendy Beats me.
Colin There's no known medical reason why he is alive. Verdict of the local doctor.
Eileen Put a great burden, of course, on you.
Colin (*moving away*) I don't think so.
Eileen The only son. (*She watches him*) How's America?
Colin Fine.
Eileen I got your card.
Colin Good.
Wendy Never sent me one.
Colin I did.
Wendy I never received it.

Pause

Colin Perhaps I didn't. (*He sits, abstracted*) I intended writing a letter. (*He exchanges a look with Wendy. Then:*) Bloody freezing up there last night. There's no heating in that bedroom.
Wendy Did you tell them you were coming up?
Colin I didn't.
Eileen None of us did.
Wendy We've never got on well. Two by two, but not the three of us together.
Colin We've hardly had the chance.
Wendy Once or twice.
Eileen I suppose it's true. Wendy and you: me and you.
Colin Wendy's mercurial. You're phlegmatic. Me: saturnine.

They laugh

Eileen Remember the occasion when father said we'd have been much better if we'd reversed the sexes?
Wendy I don't think Colin was cut out to be a woman.
Eileen You were cut out to be a man.
Wendy Me?
Eileen Me, too.
Wendy I never wished it.
Eileen Neither have I.
Wendy I'm looking forward to living on my own. Or maybe, our Eileen, with another chap.
Eileen Young or old?
Wendy Young.
Eileen How young?
Wendy Very. See what you've been missing, love.
Eileen Poor old Jack isn't all that bad.
Wendy Got his headship?
Eileen He will never get a headship. A head of department is all he'll rise to.
Wendy How about Colin?
Colin My career took a leap backwards with *The Last Evangelist*. A readership might come up in two or three years. "Too close to popular

mythology and not enough to scholarship." My Professor. *Swainton.* "It surprises me to see, nowadays, Pasmore, what they can do with popular biography."

Eileen laughs

Some mornings I set off for college, get there, return home, and I can't recall a word I've said. I assume I've passed the day in a normal way: when I go back the following day, there's no sign that I haven't. The other morning I woke so terrified that all I could do was cry for help: in the middle of a bedroom, in a quiet house, in the middle of a sedate neighbourhood near the heart of London. Kay called her doctor. I sat clinging to a chair. When you're in the grip of this thing every second becomes an hour. And then, in the wake of this feeling, comes despair.

Pasmore comes out of his room in suit, shirt and socks, carrying his shoes

He goes to the kitchen and gets cleaning materials from a cupboard. He looks round for somewhere to clean the shoes

He goes out of the back door

I'd gone to New York hoping to distract it. The opportunity came up when they publicized the book. I kept gazing out of the window, on the plane, wanting it to crash. I could see the ocean—like flecks of dust on a pane of glass—each fleck the crest of an Atlantic roller. At one point, I saw an irregular shape of the intensest white enclosing a second irregular shape of opalescent green—gleaming, iridescent—and suspended, or so it seemed, midway between the aircraft and the sea. The fear went from me. Moments after that I felt ecstatic. An iceberg, a pool of water melting at its centre. In New York I'd walk up and down outside my hotel not knowing who or where I was. I'd go into a bar, order a meal, sit over it, and, without having touched it, get up and leave. One Sunday, I sat on a flight of steps near Central Park: joggers ran past, a man sold secondhand books from a stall. I couldn't move. I sat transfixed—gripped by a dementia which even now I couldn't describe.

The bedroom door opens and Mrs Pasmore comes out dressed for an outing, but with her stick and a coat and handbag over her other arm. She is aware of the back door being open and, seeing Pasmore's door open, too, she calls:

Mrs Pasmore Tommy?
Pasmore (*off*) Out here.
Mrs Pasmore Have you got a handkerchief? (*She has one in her hands. She goes to the kitchen and checks the switches of the kettle and stove*)
Colin Why I let that out I've no idea. You get careless, at times, about how you feel.
Eileen What did the doctor say?
Colin There's not a great deal he can do. After a while, I sobered up. I go to work. I give out notes. There was a time when I couldn't work at all. I'd walk the streets. Or weep. Not through despair, you know, but terror.

Mrs Pasmore (*glancing out of the back door*) Never mind talking to Mrs Halliday. (*Calling*) He was supposed to be cleaning his shoes. (*Pause*) Tell him, love. He takes no notice of me. (*She looks at the tiny watch on her wrist*) Come in, then. (*Calling*) Thank you, love.

Pasmore comes in past her

You've been standing out there in your socks.
Pasmore (*aware he has his shoes in his hand*) I had no time to put them on.
Mrs Pasmore You've had time to talk to Mrs Halliday.
Pasmore She asked me.
Mrs Pasmore She's usually at her shop by now.
Pasmore She's on her way.
Mrs Pasmore Are you leaving all those cleaning things out there?
Pasmore Oh, yes.

He goes to retrieve them

Mrs Pasmore Too busy talking.
Pasmore (*off*) It's t' on'y chance I get.

He brings in the shoe-cleaning material in a box and puts it away in the cupboard

Mrs Pasmore And wash your hands.
Pasmore Aye.
Mrs Pasmore And put your shoes on.
Pasmore Shoes.
Mrs Pasmore Before you wash your hands.
Pasmore By God. How would I live without you?
Mrs Pasmore (*indicating the handkerchief*) I'll put this in your pocket.

Pasmore continues putting on his shoes. Mrs Pasmore goes to the living-room

Eileen Lovely, Mother.
Mrs Pasmore Thank you, love.
Pasmore (*calling*) Are you ready for off?
Wendy We are, old man!
Pasmore (*calling*) I shan't be a minute. (*He goes to the sink to wash his hands, murmuring to himself:*) "Wash hands, wash feet, wash nose."
Mrs Pasmore Is that the time? (*She checks the clock on the mantelpiece with her watch*)

Pasmore barely rinses his hands and dries them. He uses a towel, after glancing up to see if he's observed, to give his shoes a final polish. He ducks to the window to see his reflection; he can't. He smooths down his hair with one hand. He hangs up the towel and dusts it down to obviate stains

He's like a child. (*To Colin*) His second childhood, love.
Eileen You look lovely, love. (*She gives Mrs Pasmore a kiss*)
Mrs Pasmore I can't tell you how much it means to us. To see you all together. (*Calling*) Tommy!

Pasmore I'm coming. I'm coming. God damn and blast! Do this, do that, do t'other. Yes you shall. Oh no you shan't . . . Where's this, where's that, where's t'other?
Mrs Pasmore Tommy!
Pasmore I am coming. (*He takes a last look at the kitchen, and finally puts the towel in the cupboard, closes the kitchen door, and comes through. To himself*) God Christ. (*Then, entering*) How am I looking?
Wendy You're looking grand!
Eileen Lovely.
Wendy Champion! (*She kisses him*)
Colin I'll get my coat.

Colin goes to the stairs, and exits

Pasmore (*to Mrs Pasmore*) Let me help you on with yours.
Mrs Pasmore Thank you, love.
Eileen Get the glad rags on!
Wendy (*who has watched Colin depart*) Right.
Eileen Remember the church dances we used to go to?
Wendy *You* used to go to. I used to follow.
Eileen You were always popular, love. (*To Mrs Pasmore*) Used to ask me who my sister was.
Wendy One of her chums would come across: fists like melons, feet to match. "Can I have this 'un, lovely?"
Eileen Everyone was awed by Wendy. Brilliant at sport, brilliant at maths.
Wendy Changed when I got married.
Eileen Arnold!
Wendy Oh, Arnold!

Wendy and Eileen laugh

Mrs Pasmore I don't see why.

Pasmore departs to the hall for his coat

Wendy Under-manager at the age of thiry-one. Managing director at forty-five.
Eileen The boy-wonder of Maccleswade Grammar.
Wendy Chairman of the Board at forty-seven.
Mrs Pasmore *Is* he Chairman of the Board?
Wendy It's then he began casting round, our Mother, for a younger wife.
Mrs Pasmore It can't be that.
Wendy And me for a younger husband.
Mrs Pasmore Really, love. Your father doesn't know you're pulling his leg.

Pasmore returns with his coat

Pasmore It's been a house of women. I just earned the money. Come home exhausted: yak, yak. Ten to the dozen. If women could work as much as they talk, this house would be stacked to the roof with money.
Wendy It is stacked to the roof.
Pasmore What with?

Act I, Scene 2

Eileen Affection. (*She embraces him and kisses his cheek*)
Pasmore Words! I never know where I am. (*He is pleased by their attention, flustered*)
Eileen Live here like a king.
Pasmore I don't know about a king: she queens it over me enough. Do this. Do that. Yes, your majesty. My *beloved*.
Mrs Pasmore Put your coat on.
Pasmore Right!
Wendy I'll hold it for you.
Pasmore Thank you, love. Right!

The sounds of Colin coming downstairs

Are we ready?
Wendy Ready!
Eileen Ready! (*She gives Pasmore a kiss*) Mother?
Mrs Pasmore Yes, love.
Pasmore Looks a picture. Just like when I first saw her.

Colin enters with his coat, dropping it in a chair

Your car, Colin?
Colin Right.
Mrs Pasmore Through the country.
Pasmore Just fancy a drink.
Mrs Pasmore I hope you're not going to embarrass us.
Pasmore I've never embarrassed anyone.
Mrs Pasmore The last time we celebrated anything, Colin had to carry you upstairs.
Pasmore I was tired.
Mrs Pasmore Tired! (*To Eileen*) Our fiftieth wedding anniversary, love.
Pasmore We're off. Ladies before gentlemen.
Eileen Off we go, Mother.
Colin I'll lock the back door. (*He goes to the kitchen*)
Mrs Pasmore Bring out the front-door key, love. Put the fireguard round.
Pasmore It's on. It's on. (*He does so*)
Mrs Pasmore (*to Eileen*) A mother's instinct, love.
Pasmore We're off!

Mrs Pasmore leads the way to the front door. It is heard to open

Pasmore follows

Wendy indicates for Eileen to go before her

Eileen After you, our kid.
Wendy (*calling*) Colin!

Eileen and Wendy go

Colin (*calling*) Right! (*He locks the back door, bolts it and chains it. He comes back to the living-room, picks up the coat he's dropped there and looks round at the room*)

Wendy (*off*) Colin!
Eileen (*off*) Colin!

Colin pulls himself together, starts to put on the coat, and goes

The sound of the front door closing and the key being turned is heard

Pasmore (*further off*) Come and get this car unlocked.
Colin (*calling, off*) Right!
Eileen (*off, fainter*) Colin!
Wendy (*off, fainter still*) Colin!

The Lights fade to black-out

ACT II

Scene 1

The same. Evening

Evening light at the window and the low glow of the fire

The front door is unlocked

Mrs Pasmore (*off*) You had a peggy-stick. It had three legs, like a stool, with a broom-handle, and you thrashed it up and down. My arms! They used to ache!

She comes into sight in the passage, from the front door

Sometimes the clothes would get wound up, more with the handle than anything else—(*She goes into the living-room*)

Eileen follows her, switching on the light

—then you'd have to reach into the tub. The water we'd heat in a copper and ladle it out with a metal jug. That took some time: *emptying* the tub with buckets. I used to be that exhausted I'd sit on the stairs and cry. (*She gasps and holds her chest*) My breath! I could never catch it! (*She lays down her handbag, suddenly conscious of the room*) When you were young the buckets were heavier than you could handle: so much would spill on the floor.

She allows Eileen to help her off with her coat

Then the mopping-up.

Wendy comes in the front door and along the passage. She carries a box of chocolates

We'd be wet through at times. (*She catches sight of Wendy entering*) When Wendy was old enough, she'd pitch in. Those *were* wash-days! When it rained—a house of clothes for the better part of two days drying round the fire.

Wendy (*to Eileen*) Your car keys, love. (*To Mrs Pasmore*) There's your chocolates. (*She hands them to Eileen to give to Mrs Pasmore*)

Eileen Mother: your box of chocolates.

Mrs Pasmore Thank you, love. (*She kisses her*) What a lovely picture. Almond blossom.

Eileen Cherry.

Wendy Plum.

Mrs Pasmore I couldn't eat another thing. That meal went on for hours. I'll just put on the kettle.
Wendy I'll do it, Mother.
Mrs Pasmore Mend up the fire. I shan't be a minute. (*She goes to the kitchen*) There you are. (*She switches on the kitchen light*)

Pasmore comes in, rather slow on his feet

Eileen You poke. I'll shove on the fuel.

Wendy removes the fireguard and pokes the fire. Eileen lifts the scuttle and tips on the coal

Pasmore (*at the living-room door, pausing*) Women working. Don't often see it nowadays.
Wendy Nowadays, Father, you see nothing else.
Pasmore This house, lass, I'm talking about. (*He covers his mouth, glancing back to the kitchen*)

Mrs Pasmore is in the kitchen filling the kettle. She plugs it in, then re-straightens the curtains. She washes her hands during the following action

Wendy You were bad enough in the restaurant, Dad.
Pasmore Can't stomach well-dressed people.
Eileen You're well-dressed.
Pasmore I'm only well-dressed when I'm going out with you. (*He puts his arm round Wendy and kisses her cheek*) Thy's putting on some weight.
Wendy I am not.
Pasmore Eileen was as plump as a chicken. Thy'd disappear inside your clothes and we'd never know you wa' theer. How are you, Eileen?
Eileen Champion, Dad. (*She gives him a kiss*)
Pasmore Grand meal.
Eileen It was.
Pasmore Even if Colin paid for it.
Wendy We all paid for it, Father. Except you.
Pasmore The exception that proves the rule!
Eileen That's right.

Having washed her hands, Mrs Pasmore has gone to dry them but the towel is not there. She looks round and finally locates it in the cupboard

Mrs Pasmore (*to herself*) Where's that towel?
Wendy Where's Colin?
Pasmore Locking up his car.
Eileen Bought it with the money from his book.
Pasmore Nothing beats hard work. Motto of my life. That fire could do with poking.
Wendy I've poked it.
Pasmore You've dabbed at it. God Christ! (*He pokes the fire himself*) This fire and me are close together. I often talk to this on a morning. "How are you?" "I'm fine." "Want a bit o' feeding?" "Right!" A house wi'out a fire is like a home wi'out a woman.

Act II, Scene 1   37

Mrs Pasmore Have you seen this?

Pasmore turns as Mrs Pasmore comes in, holding up the towel which she has extracted from the cupboard

Pasmore What is it?
Mrs Pasmore It's a towel.
Pasmore A towel.
Mrs Pasmore From the kitchen.
Pasmore The kitchen.
Mrs Pasmore Just look at it!
Eileen It's only a towel, Mother.
Mrs Pasmore It's my towel, love. That's polish.
Pasmore I had an accident.
Mrs Pasmore An accident!
Pasmore If I've muckied it, I thought, I'll give 'em a little rub.
Mrs Pasmore You've used it on your shoes!
Pasmore (*holding one foot out, then the other*) Can see yourself in that.
Mrs Pasmore After all these years! It'll never come off. (*She weeps*) He has his own towel in the bathroom. I don't know what he does with his hands.
Pasmore I make the fire. I empty it every two or three days.
Mrs Pasmore It's too much. (*She sits*) I keep the house clean. All he does is dirty it up.

Colin comes in, closing the front door and emerging in the passage. He now stands in the living-room doorway

Wendy (*with her arm round Mrs Pasmore's shoulder*) You're surely not going to get upset?
Mrs Pasmore I'll never use it again.

Wendy takes it from her

Eileen You'll wash it.
Mrs Pasmore It'll never come out. It's too much.
Pasmore Are we having us some tea or aren't we?
Wendy I'll put it on.
Mrs Pasmore (*calling*) Don't put that towel with the washing.
Wendy (*going*) Why not?
Mrs Pasmore It needs special rinsing.
Colin What's the problem?
Wendy Towel. (*She holds it up as she passes him in the door*)
Eileen Dad has used mother's towel to polish his shoes.
Pasmore A final flick. It fell on the floor. I must have put on too much polish.
Mrs Pasmore It never fell.
Pasmore How do you know what it did?
Mrs Pasmore You picked up the closest thing to hand. The story of my life.
Pasmore Like I picked up you, you mean?
Mrs Pasmore *You never picked me up!* You never did!

Pasmore I don't know where I am. Go out and celebrate and we end up here in tears.
Mrs Pasmore It's your thoughtlessness. Your never counting what comes next. It was me who made this family. Saving every week. Penny after penny.
Pasmore I'm off to bed.
Mrs Pasmore You'll do no such thing.
Pasmore I'll run off wi' Mrs Halliday to her boutique.
Mrs Pasmore You'd like that, I know.
Pasmore Life at the seaside, Colin!
Mrs Pasmore We're not at the seaside. We're in the country. I couldn't live in a seaside town. (*To Colin*) It's far too crowded in the summer.
Pasmore Autumn now.
Mrs Pasmore I don't care when it is.

Pause

Wendy makes tea and arranges a tray in the kitchen. She has put the towel in the empty washing-machine

Pasmore A towel isn't that imporant.
Mrs Pasmore It is to me.
Pasmore I'll buy you another. As it is, I've bought you this. (*He gives her a box from his pocket*)
Mrs Pasmore What is it?
Pasmore Open it and see.
Mrs Pasmore Well, I don't know...
Eileen Open it, Mother.
Mrs Pasmore Well... (*She gazes at it*)
Colin Open it.
Eileen (*calling*) Wendy!

Wendy, in the kitchen, pauses

Colin Wendy!
Eileen (*calling*) Come and look at this!

Wendy comes back through. Pasmore shifts his position to another chair

Father's given Mother a present.
Wendy That's quick. He was in the doghouse a minute ago.
Eileen Well, then, Mother...
Mrs Pasmore Are you ready?
Pasmore We're ready.

Mrs Pasmore opens the box

Mrs Pasmore You might have chosen a better moment.
Pasmore When?
Mrs Pasmore Sooner rather than later.
Pasmore The restaurant, I thought, wa' far too crowded.
Mrs Pasmore It's lovely, love. What is it?

Pasmore A ring.
Mrs Pasmore A ring. (*She puts it on*) It's made to fit a giant.
Pasmore They'll alter it.
Mrs Pasmore Where did you get it?
Pasmore What does it matter?
Wendy Let's have a look.
Mrs Pasmore It looks like a brooch.
Eileen Let's have a look, Mother.
Wendy It is a brooch.
Eileen No, it isn't.
Mrs Pasmore Can you see it, Colin?
Colin It looks grand.
Pasmore I've been saving up for that.
Mrs Pasmore Where did you get the money?
Pasmore I've saved it.
Mrs Pasmore You haven't spent our contingency fund?
Pasmore What contingency fund?
Mrs Pasmore For our funeral!
Eileen You've not been saving up for that?
Mrs Pasmore Everybody did in our day, love. Sometimes not more than a halfpenny a week.
Pasmore I haven't touched it. You'll be buried when you dee. I'll be buried. We'll all be buried.
Mrs Pasmore Where did you get it?
Pasmore It's a present. What is this place? A prison?
Wendy Why don't you say thank you, love?
Mrs Pasmore Thank you.
Pasmore Theer, then.
Mrs Pasmore Let me give you a kiss.
Pasmore If you think that I deserve it.
Mrs Pasmore Of course you deserve it. (*She holds both arms out*)

Pasmore crosses to her, leans down and is kissed

There. You see. It's already dropped off.
Wendy I'll get it, Mother.
Mrs Pasmore Where he's got it from ...
Pasmore Where do you think I got it?
Mrs Pasmore I'm sure I couldn't guess.
Colin (*having picked it up*) Gold. (*He examines it*)
Pasmore He's the same, you see.
Mrs Pasmore It's such an unusual ring.
Pasmore An antique.
Mrs Pasmore Did you buy it secondhand?
Pasmore It has a motto.
Colin "From E.T to U.N."
Wendy It's a "B".
Mrs Pasmore It is secondhand.
Colin "Amo ..."

Pasmore It means "I love".
Wendy Who's "B.T."?
Eileen Who's "U.N."?
Pasmore In latin.
Wendy "Te Amo".
Pasmore "I love you."
Mrs Pasmore (*taking it back in her outstretched hand*) It is secondhand. (*She examines it*)
Pasmore It doesn't make any difference.
Mrs Pasmore It's like someone else's clothes.
Pasmore I wanted to buy you a present.
Mrs Pasmore You could have bought me flowers.
Pasmore Flowers don't last.
Mrs Pasmore I'd never let one of these wear someone else's clothes. I'd stay up all night mending rather than take in someone else's rejects. (*She puts the ring back in its box*)
Pasmore That's not a reject.
Colin For God's sake, Mother: he's bought you a present.
Mrs Pasmore Like all his presents, Colin
Pasmore That's not true.
Wendy Not true at all.
Mrs Pasmore Not all his presents. Just like some. (*She takes out her handkerchief*)
Pasmore What did I have to buy you ought?
Mrs Pasmore You had your pension.
Pasmore You look after that.
Mrs Pasmore You could have asked.
Pasmore I did. (*He sits and weeps bitterly to himself*)
Eileen There's the kettle.
Colin I'll get it. (*He goes to the kitchen*)
Wendy The two of you behave. Both of you say sorry.
Mrs Pasmore If I give him too much he goes and spends it. He has to be watched. I can't let your father out of my sight. On those fruit machines. As well as something else.
Eileen Now what is it? What's been happening?
Mrs Pasmore It's nothing that I want to talk about. I'll take the ring. I appreciate the thought. I mean that.
Wendy I'll get the tea. (*She goes to the kitchen and signals to Colin to return to the living-room. She finishes the tea-making and setting the tray*)
Colin (*returning*) Sorted it all out?
Mrs Pasmore There's nothing to sort out, love.
Pasmore All fine and dandy. (*He blows his nose*) All a picture.
Mrs Pasmore Getting old: it has its problems. It's true for everyone, I suppose.
Pasmore (*blowing his nose*) I thought of buying flowers. Then I saw that. Amo means I love. *Te Amo* means I love you. (*He weeps into his hand*)

Pause

Act II, Scene 1   41

Colin There's no need to get upset about it, Dad.
Pasmore It's just today. You all being here.
Mrs Pasmore We hadn't a farthing when we married.
Pasmore We wouldn't have now if it wasn't for these.
Mrs Pasmore Neither of Tommy's parents came to our wedding. Mine thought I should have stayed at home. All my sisters and brothers were working or married. The youngest in those days had to help around the house.
Pasmore A domestic servant.
Mrs Pasmore Your brothers came.
Pasmore Four. Four of 'em came, and eight of 'em not.
Mrs Pasmore None of your sisters.
Pasmore None of my sisters.
Mrs Pasmore The church was a bowling-alley last time I saw it.
Pasmore When we got on the train for the honeymoon I had to stand. She sat i' the carriage, next to a chap who chatted to her all the way.
Mrs Pasmore He was very handsome.
Pasmore A square moustache, eyes as big as saucers, flushed cheeks. I went in a time or two and said, "Are you all right?"
Mrs Pasmore I was all right.
Pasmore Would you believe it? The fourth or fifth time I went in this chap said, "Is this man troubling you, my dear?"
Wendy (*coming in with the tray and hearing this*) What did you tell him?
Mrs Pasmore I said he was!

They laugh

Eileen Why didn't you tell him he was your husband?
Mrs Pasmore I was too embarrassed.
Pasmore Embarrassed!
Mrs Pasmore I hardly knew anything about the world. I was nineteen. I'd worked in a mill before my mother asked me to help at home. Tommy was the first man I ever went out with. (*She pulls her skirt over her knees*) If a young woman couldn't be spoken to by a young man on a crowded train, I don't see where else she could be spoken to. He was very polite. "Is this man pestering you?" he said.
Pasmore He asked, at the other end, if he could carry her case.
Mrs Pasmore I don't know why you didn't let him. Thank you, love. (*She takes a cup of tea from Wendy*)
Pasmore If it's not been one man, it's been another. (*He takes a cup of tea from Wendy*) Thank you.
Mrs Pasmore I can't help it if I'm attractive.
Pasmore With a walking-stick?
Mrs Pasmore You should have seen him oggle me in my costume.
Pasmore God Christ, it was longer than a nightdress. "Do you think I should show my ankles?" You couldn't even see her bloody toes! (*He laughs; and then chokes, holding his tea. He drinks*)
Mrs Pasmore This is a conversation to have in front of our children.

Pasmore If they are our children. From what you're telling us, they might only be yours.
Mrs Pasmore He doesn't know when to stop. He carries a joke too far.
Colin When you were married, where did you live?
Mrs Pasmore We lived in a room at my mother's.
Pasmore About the size o' that kitchen. A street, tha knows, at the back of a mill.
Eileen Thank you. (*She takes a cup of tea from Wendy*)
Mrs Pasmore We had a bed against one wall.
Pasmore One cupboard.
Mrs Pasmore One chair.
Pasmore A window the size of a matchbox.
Mrs Pasmore It was.
Pasmore In the middle of summer you had to burn candles to see where you were.
Mrs Pasmore Water from a tap in the yard outside.
Pasmore We had to wash in the basement.
Mrs Pasmore We had Eileen at that time.
Pasmore Aye.
Mrs Pasmore The Council came one morning—Tommy was working nights and asleep in bed. I was washing Eileen in a little bath. They took one look at this tiny room and said, "We'll get you a home, Mrs Pasmore."
Pasmore Got us a council house after that.
Mrs Pasmore A godsend.
Pasmore A palace.
Eileen You don't have to tell us, Mother.
Mrs Pasmore No. No. Of course. That's right.
Pasmore Today's been one to remember.
Mrs Pasmore It has. (*Looking at the clock, then her watch*) Must have been eight hours.
Pasmore Six.
Mrs Pasmore That ride over the moor. I don't think I've been that route before.
Wendy Good job you told them at the restaurant it was you arriving, Dad.
Pasmore They know me there by now.
Mrs Pasmore We've never been there in our lives.
Pasmore Nay, about town.
Mrs Pasmore You've hardly been into town without me.
Pasmore I've been a time or two on my own.
Mrs Pasmore He talks to anybody. You, me: out it comes. All about his children. Colin's book. Wendy's council. Eileen's children.
Wendy Something to be proud of.
Pasmore That's what I tell her. She never listens.
Mrs Pasmore He spoke to one man one morning and the man said, "Are you trying to solicit me?"
Pasmore He was mad.
Mrs Pasmore He said he'd call the police.

Act II, Scene 1 43

Pasmore All I said to him was, "How are you going?" He said, "Are you trying to . . ." What was the word?
Mrs Pasmore Solicit.
Pasmore Harmless. (*He drinks tea*)
Mrs Pasmore I've never seen you move off as quick as that.
Pasmore I'll be buggered if I'm had up for being a homosexual.
Mrs Pasmore He's been had up for a lot of things.
Colin What things?
Mrs Pasmore Matches. (*She watches Pasmore*)
Pasmore Matches.
Mrs Pasmore He had matches down the pit.
Pasmore Three.
Mrs Pasmore We had to come back from our honeymoon for him to appear in court.
Pasmore Ten shillings for every match.
Mrs Pasmore It was more than he earned each week.
Wendy How did you pay them back?
Pasmore A bob a week.
Mrs Pasmore Thirty shillings altogether.
Pasmore An accident! I'd forgotten all about them.
Mrs Pasmore Endangering lives.
Pasmore Endangering nothing.
Mrs Pasmore Why did they have you up in court?
Pasmore If I had a pound for every man I've seen with a matchbox down the pit, I'd be the richest man alive. I'd have summat on my back you could call a coat.
Mrs Pasmore That is a good coat. I bought you that last Christmas.
Pasmore It's a very good coat.
Mrs Pasmore In that case, why disparage it?
Pasmore If you have bought it, my love, it's good enough for me.
Mrs Pasmore He doesn't know when he's well looked after.
Pasmore I do. I do. After all these years.
Mrs Pasmore Fancy giving me a present with someone else's inscription.
Eileen It's not worth going into, Mother.
Mrs Pasmore It's typical, love. He could have bought me something.
Wendy Have you bought him something?
Mrs Pasmore Why should I?
Wendy You don't have to sit there and let it all come to you.
Mrs Pasmore Let what come to me?
Wendy Openness. Generosity. Strength.

Pause

Mrs Pasmore You were never very fond of me.
Wendy I am very fond of you. I love you. I always have.
Mrs Pasmore There are feelings and feelings.
Wendy Are there?
Mrs Pasmore I shan't say any more. (*She draws her skirt over her knees*) Certainly not on a day like this.

Wendy What have we to hide?
Mrs Pasmore What have we, indeed?
Wendy You haven't anything, Colin?
Colin I don't believe I have.
Wendy Eileen?
Eileen None of your usual habits.
Wendy What habits.
Mrs Pasmore As a child she was always stirring up things that were better left alone. (*To Eileen*) That's why she became a politician.
Wendy That's right. I did. What's the point of leaving anything alone? Particularly the way things are at present.
Mrs Pasmore Or are some people so born to mischief that they won't leave things alone in order to damage others?
Pasmore I'll go get out of these clothes. (*He rises*) I'm not used to being in a suit (*He staggers*)
Eileen You've had too much to drink.
Pasmore A little goes a long way in my book. Any road, (*he starts to leave*) each day is a celebration. You being here, tha knows, is good enough for me. (*He coughs*)

Pasmore goes out of the room

Eileen (*to Wendy*) You've driven him off.
Pasmore (*popping back in the doorway*) As for drinking: it wasn't me that drank a bottle of wine. Don't look at our Colin. He was driving. Your mother and I had a glass of champagne.
Wendy A bit before, old man.
Pasmore A drop. A drop.

He closes the living-room door and goes to his bedroom. He opens the door and goes in, but doesn't completely close it

Mrs Pasmore I think I'll go and lie down.
Eileen Do you want any help, Mother?
Mrs Pasmore No thank you, love.

Colin holds the door for her.

Mrs Pasmore goes. She opens her bedroom door, goes inside and closes it

Eileen You've had too much to drink.
Wendy I had sufficient.
Eileen Why spoil a lovely day?
Wendy Why, indeed? (*She sits*) Aren't you going to say anything, Colin?
Colin Not much.

Mrs Pasmore comes out of her room and goes to the living room

Wendy No wonder he writes a book about an evangelical who blew up half the industrialized world and retires into an academic shell the next.
Mrs Pasmore I worked hard all my life. I brought up all of you on next to nothing, with a husband who had an eye for women like he had for nothing else, and who drank when I first knew him.

Wendy He was a very good father.
Mrs Pasmore You don't know the half of it. You don't know your father, love, at all.
Wendy I know he coughed his guts out at the coal-face for the better part of fifty years. What did you do, Mother?
Mrs Pasmore She always had a vicious streak. (*To Eileen*) You can see what I had to put up with. If she gets it from anyone it's not from me.
Wendy Your life was no harder, Mother, than that of many women, and a good deal easier than most. I have women in my office every day of every week begging for guidance, begging for peace. Broken in mind, broken in spirit. *Broke*. With homes that reek like sewers, with minds racked by anxiety and depression—and by a hatred which, if you brought it into this room, would set this place alight. I do my job as best I can. I get no satisfaction—except that of knowing that, if *I* didn't do it, someone else might do it worse.
Mrs Pasmore It seems to me, my dear, you are full of despair.
Wendy So are you. But mine, my dear, is on the move.
Eileen What's got into you, our kid?
Colin It's better, far better she lets it out.
Eileen Is it? Is it? Aren't some things, Colin, better left unsaid?
Mrs Pasmore (*sitting weeping*) Don't you think I haven't despaired? Don't you think I haven't been full of it myself? Day after day. Most women from our neighbourhood never raised their sights higher than the local pub. I did. I'd have given anything to have been able to get out of the house. When you were children, your father's wage was four pounds ten. No matter how hard I struggled, I couldn't get our housekeeping lower than five. New shoes would throw my budget out for months. A new suit would throw it out for years. I baked, I cooked, I cleaned, I sewed. To wash your father's clothes took half a day. My father was a farrier. His trade was in decline. He was wounded in the war. He could scarcely stoop to shoe a horse. I saw him try. He had a bullet through his lungs. I loved him. Oh, I loved him! (*She weeps*) He never complained. Not once. Never! (*She weeps bitterly into her hands*) He was a saint. A *saint*! (*Pause*) You were married to a managing director. You have a lovely house, on the edge of a wood. I'm not saying it's cost you nothing—but nothing to the price that some of us have had to pay. (*She covers her face in her hands*)

Wendy moves to the door of the living-room, which has been left open from Mrs Pasmore's entrance

Wendy (*calling*) You can come out of there, old man.

Pause

Pasmore's bedroom door is finally drawn back. Pasmore comes out, white-faced, perhaps the effect of too much drink—though not otherwise apparent—and of what he has heard through the open door. He has changed into trousers, an open-necked shirt and a pullover, his hair ruffled. He, too, behind the door has wept

Are you all right?

Pasmore Grand! (*He rubs his hands together*)
Eileen Do you want more tea?
Pasmore No thanks. (*He comes in with a fearful look to Wendy*)
Wendy It's unusual, with our domestic arrangements, that we get the chance to come together. In most families that I know of, the brothers and sisters are out of touch.
Eileen Aren't you casting round with a flail?
Wendy A flail?
Eileen Because you've lost your husband.
Wendy Husbands may, my dear, be everything to you. They are nothing at all to me.
Eileen And children?
Wendy Children?
Eileen You haven't any, Wendy.
Wendy I've tried.
Eileen And didn't succeed.
Wendy Alkaline douches, I'm afraid, didn't do the trick. Nether did sexual positioning, temperature graphs, or artificial insemination—techniques which, in my case, came too late. Ten years younger, our kid, I might have had a child. How about you? What do you do that's so important?
Eileen I go out to work.
Wendy Do you?
Eileen Part time.
Colin Eristic argument: it used to dominate our house. It's what often drove me out of it.
Mrs Pasmore What's "eristic"?
Wendy Two down: seven letter word.
Colin Arguing not to establish a truth but for effect. I have no time for it. I never had.
Eileen (*speaking generally*) More tea?
Pasmore No thanks.

Pasmore shakes his head, the only one to respond

Wendy Eileen always thought you went out as our protagonist, Colin. Our crusader. The heathen being anyone our parents took an exception to.
Mrs Pasmore We sent him out to better himself.
Wendy Did you better it, Colin? This self you never knew you had. Or did you half destroy it?
Mrs Pasmore We gave you all an education. The best there was to have.
Wendy I see Colin labouring night after night: Latin, Greek, Maths, History. Ah, *History*! I had to forego a dress, Eileen a skirt, our mother a coat. Science. Art. When I followed him all I saw was Colin's back, *heaving*. "Every shovelful of coal I dig, I dig it out for you." Isn't that what you used to tell him, Dad? I never felt it, of course, myself. Digging out a spadeful for a daughter didn't carry the same weight as it did for a son. Nevertheless, I made it count. I made it count.
Pasmore He had a better life than me.

Act II, Scene 1   47

Wendy Has he? Did he? (*She looks at Colin*) It wasn't enlightenment they were shaping you towards, but work conducted from a sitting position, equated with a profession, not a job, with a salary, not a wage.
Colin It wasn't that.
Wendy What was it, Colin?
Colin (*to Mrs Pasmore*) Do you remember how you used to say you never embraced me as a child?
Mrs Pasmore As a *baby*.
Colin I wonder why.
Mrs Pasmore I always thought if you had too much cuddling you'd grow up soft. I cuddled Eileen, of course, a lot. And Wendy. She used to cuddle me. She was always cuddling. You were always very cuddly, love.
Wendy Yet never Colin.
Mrs Pasmore He didn't seem to want it, love!
Wendy As a baby?
Mrs Pasmore As a boy. I used to let him lie.
Wendy What for?
Mrs Pasmore I wasn't very sure of men. I was always blushing when the rentman came.
Pasmore What did I tell you! What did I say!
Mrs Pasmore It was modesty, that's all. With Tommy working shifts, I was often alone in the house at night.
Wendy Our father helped when he was there.
Mrs Pasmore He was very fond of all of you. With Colin he always fought. On his knees. In front of the fire. With you two, of course, it was always games. Hiding and chasing. You used to love it. There it is. The joys and tribulations.
Eileen It's not a great deal, to go by default.
Wendy Default?
Eileen When you measure it against their virtues.
Wendy Virtues?
Eileen *Strengths!*
Mrs Pasmore After all, you were all three loved!
Wendy Loved!
Mrs Pasmore Believe me: I never meant you, nor Colin, nor Eileen, any harm.
Wendy Dad?

Pasmore shakes his head

Eileen (*to Colin*) Are you all right?
Colin I'm fine. (*He glances at Eileen, then turns away*) I'm grand!

Pause

Mrs Pasmore And what of your father?
Eileen What about him?
Mrs Pasmore If you have your traumas, what of his?
Colin What are your traumas, Dad?
Pasmore Never you mind.

Wendy Out with it, Dad.
Pasmore On with the dance!
Mrs Pasmore If everything's coming out, it might as well.
Pasmore It's nowt.
Mrs Pasmore Nothing!
Pasmore To make a fuss.
Mrs Pasmore He's been stealing from a shop.
Pasmore I pick things up. I can't remember.
Mrs Pasmore He puts things in his pocket. A life of honesty thrown away. We've never taken a penny—not a halfpenny—not from anyone. We've always paid our way. Now this.
Wendy Why didn't anyone tell us?
Mrs Pasmore He asked me not to. You've got your troubles. We've got ours.
Pasmore It's nowt.
Mrs Pasmore The shopkeeper said he'd take him to court. The local shop. The only one we've got.
Pasmore I shan't ever show my face again. (*To Mrs Pasmore*) I told you it was coming.
Mrs Pasmore How did you tell me?
Pasmore I said I didn't feel well. I had a headache whenever I went in.
Mrs Pasmore I have a headache whenever I go in. But not because I steal.
Colin You've been left too much on your own up here.
Mrs Pasmore Wendy's too busy. Eileen has her lads. You're in London.
Colin I'll come up here more often.
Wendy I'll come over. (*To Eileen*) We'll both come over. (*To Pasmore*) It's nothing to go on about.
Pasmore It is to me.
Mrs Pasmore He doesn't sleep at night for worry.
Pasmore I'll go to prison.
Wendy You will not.
Pasmore I've read cases in the paper.
Eileen You're not giving in after all these years?
Pasmore In?
Wendy Fighting, Father!
Pasmore It's not fighting, lass. It's nought I understand.
Wendy Have you seen the doctor?
Mrs Pasmore Doctor?
Wendy You don't think he's a thief? He needs someone he can talk to.
Pasmore I got up thinking this was a special day. I bought that ring.
Mrs Pasmore Where did you get it?
Pasmore I got it in the market.
Mrs Pasmore The market!
Pasmore He sells antiques.
Mrs Pasmore We've never bought anything from a stall in the market.
Pasmore Lots of things. Lots.
Mrs Pasmore Not as a present.

Act II, Scene 1

Pasmore shakes his head in disbelief: he can not make sense of what he feels

Pasmore I *saved* for it! I paid good money.
Mrs Pasmore What out of?
Pasmore I *saved*! (*He goes to the door*)
Mrs Pasmore And don't rush off.
Pasmore I'm not rushing off.
Mrs Pasmore I've had to sit here and take abuse.
Wendy It's not abuse.
Mrs Pasmore I've had to sit here and take criticism, haven't I?
Pasmore I don't know what's happening to me. I don't know where I am any more.
Mrs Pasmore You're at home, with your wife, your son and your daughters.
Pasmore (*to Colin*) At your age, one neet—on night-shift—I lost my head. One chap wa' going on at me. I wa' supposed to be in charge: he wa' telling me what to do—foul-mouthed, half-drunk. I said, "If you don't do what I tell you, I'll ram you through wi' this." A rock-drill: a bit as sharp as a needle and twice as long as this. (*He indicates his arm*) "Go so-and-so yourself," he said. I would have killed him. I wa're on'y half his size. I couldn't get to him. For the best part of an hour I chased him round that face. After that it wa', "Go so-and-so yourself," to everybody. To me it was, "Yes, Tommy," and "No, Tommy," and "I'll do that Tommy." He knew I'd meant it. *I* knew I'd meant it. That man came as close to deein' that night as he ever came to deein' wukking on that face. (*Indicating Mrs Pasmore*) I used to come home and fall asleep wi' the pit muck on me. I'd fall asleep at the table. Everything wa' black. It lasted two or three year. She used to say, "Whatever's happened?" I couldn't explain it. There's scarcely a day goes by when I don't feel I've ever quite got over it. I worked for every penny. I wa're at the coal-face at sixty-five . . .
Wendy I'll go see this shopkeeper and sort it out.
Pasmore All I wanted to do was buy you a present. You tell me I went and stole it.
Mrs Pasmore I asked.
Pasmore Does it make any difference? I gave him money—my money. (*He holds his head*) I wish you'd never told them. I wish to God they'd never come back.
Mrs Pasmore I'm glad they did.
Pasmore To run me down.
Mrs Pasmore To run you nothing!
Wendy All a lot about nothing.
Eileen Right!
Wendy On with the dance!
Pasmore Every tale has a happy ending.
Wendy Every?
Pasmore Almost . . .
Eileen What about this one, Father?
Pasmore I don't know. (*He shakes his head*) I don't know.

Pause

Wendy We'll get this shop business sorted out. We'll come up here more often.
Pasmore There isn't much longer for either your mother or me to go.
Wendy Quite a bit.
Pasmore Not much. Not much.
Wendy It's all the more important, in that case, to relish what we have. (*She puts her arm round Pasmore*)
Pasmore Aye ... I suppose that's true.
Wendy You don't honestly think I'm wicked, love? (*She sits on the arm of the chair beside Mrs Pasmore, putting her arm around her shoulder*)
Mrs Pasmore If you'd had a child you'd understand.
Pasmore I'm going to have a rest.
Mrs Pasmore I'll lie down, too.
Pasmore What time are you leaving?
Wendy Eileen?
Eileen I've got to get back this evening.
Wendy Me, too.
Pasmore In that case, I'd better stay up.
Eileen Lie down for an hour. We'll still be here.
Pasmore Hilda?
Mrs Pasmore I'll lie down, too.
Colin Do you want a hand?
Mrs Pasmore Thank you, love.

Colin holds her arm to the door

Pasmore How about me?
Eileen Here. I'll carry you! (*She takes his arm*)
Pasmore It'll take more than you to lift me, love. I could lift all three of you in one arm afore. How long ago is that?
Eileen A long, long time.
Pasmore If I don't wek up just let me know.
Wendy We'll wake you, Dad.

Colin and Mrs Pasmore get to her bedroom door

Colin Are you all right, Mother?
Mrs Pasmore Thank you, love. (*To Eileen*) Wake us, won't you, before you leave?
Eileen We will.

Pasmore and Mrs Pasmore go into their rooms. The bedroom doors are closed. Pause

Colin and Eileen go back into the living room. Colin closes the door

Wendy I hate driving in the dark.
Eileen I'll give Jack a ring before I leave.
Wendy You're very quiet.
Colin I'm not leaving until tomorrow.

Act II, Scene 1

Wendy I'll stay.
Colin You don't have to.
Wendy I'll ring the office. (*She indicates the bedrooms*) If they're distressed then so am I.
Eileen Do you remember your "throne"? That chair you used to stand on?
Wendy Our father used to cheer.
Eileen He'd say, "Tell us why the nationalization of the coal industry will do us all a bit of good".
Colin That went down like a bomb.
Wendy I enlightened every one of you. Him (*she indicates Colin*) and you especially.
Colin Better close the door. (*He makes sure the living-room door is closed*)
Eileen Like when father was on shifts.
Colin "Speak in whispers."
Eileen "Don't run about."
Wendy His bloody snores would wake the dead.
Eileen "Why can't we make a noise when Dad is snoring?"
Colin Precocious.
Wendy Are you staying on as well?
Eileen That's right.
Wendy I'll take these through. (*She collects the tea-things and goes to the kitchen*)
Eileen There was a time when Wendy was a hausfrau.
Colin Before Arnold got loose-handed at the office.
Eileen Was it really as bad as that?
Colin Aren't really words to describe it. Still.

Pause

Eileen Could put more coal on that.
Colin Right.
Wendy (*entering*) Found this. (*She holds up a bottle of wine*) I'll get three glasses. Keep them here. (*She stoops to the sideboard and gets glasses out*)
Eileen Don't fancy a drink.
Colin Nor do I.
Wendy I'll have one. (*She hands a glass to Colin as he rises from the fire*) Pour one out.
Colin I think I'll have one.
Wendy Eileen?
Eileen (*glancing at Colin; pause*) Right.
Wendy (*to Colin*) Three.
Colin Wake them, shall we?
Wendy No.
Eileen No.

Wendy takes her glassful, holds it up to examine it, and sips

Wendy Not bad.

Colin pours less than half into each of the other two glasses and hands one to Eileen

Here's to it.
Colin Mother and Dad. (*He toasts*)
Wendy Mother and Father.
Eileen Mother and Father.
All Mother and Father.

They drink

The light fades

SCENE 2

The same. The next day

Daylight shows through behind closed curtains; the fire has died down

Wendy, her head on a cushion, and covered by a blanket, is curled up on the settee, asleep

The light is stronger in the kitchen where the curtains are open

Colin comes downstairs, dressed. He goes to the kitchen, after drawing the living-room door to as he passes. He picks up the pot of tea steaming there, as is the kettle, and drinks

Wendy raises her head in the living-room, and looks over to the door. She rises. She stretches, goes over to the curtains, and draws them back. She flinches at the daylight

Colin, hearing sounds, pours tea into a cup from the teapot, puts in milk and sugar, and stirs it. He brings it to the door and taps on it

Wendy (*stretching*) Oh, it's you.
Colin You up?
Wendy That's very kind of you. (*She takes the cup*)
Colin Milk and sugar.
Wendy Anyone up?
Colin I've taken them a pot of tea. Remember how Eileen used to sleep with her head hooded in a blanket? Still does. Fire in. (*He picks up the bucket*)
Wendy What time are you leaving?
Colin Soon.
Wendy Have a wash.
Colin My mother put out a towel. Pink. I've told them you're still here.

He takes the bucket and goes and unlocks the back door. He goes out

Wendy goes to the bathroom and closes the door

Pasmore's door opens. He comes out in his trousers, shirt, pullover and slippers. He goes to the bathroom door and tries it

Pasmore Sorry.

Act II, Scene 2

He comes into the living-room and sits, gazing at the fireplace. He raises his head at the sound of the bucket at the back door

Colin comes in, closing the back door

Colin goes to the living-room. Pasmore rises

Colin There you are, Dad.
Pasmore Aye ...
Colin Still in. (*He indicates the fire*)
Pasmore I'll do it.
Colin No, no. Sit down.
Pasmore My job.

He sits and watches Colin rake the fire then set in pieces of coal

Concessionary coal. Pay for the haulage. Comes half-price. (*Aimlessly*) Call this "the coal-house", tha knows, round here.
Colin Sleep all right?
Pasmore Not bad. Where did you lot sleep?
Colin Eileen up. Wendy down here. I offered her my bed. She wouldn't have it.
Pasmore I thought they had to be off last night.
Colin Decided to stay over.
Pasmore It'll not burn up. (*He watches the fire*) You need to pull that shutter. Push it to the left.

Colin pushes a lever above the fire itself, let into the metalwork within the tiled façade

You can see it drawing.
Colin Were you upset last night when I came in?
Pasmore When did you come in?
Colin Before I went to bed.
Pasmore I don't remember.
Colin I didn't hear you snoring.
Pasmore I don't snore. (*He looks up in the direction of Mrs Pasmore's room*) That's put about by your mother.
Colin I've taken her a cup of tea. We have to get off, I think, quite soon.
Pasmore (*rubbing his face*) I remember scarce ought about last night. (*Pause*) I don't remember too much about this morning. (*He looks up*) I can never mek any sense on it. You look for a bit o' peace. (*He shakes his head, then bows it*) All you get is nowt and nothing.

Pause

Wendy comes out of the bathroom

Pause. She listens to the silence in the living-room then comes in

Wendy Sleep all right? (*She stoops to Pasmore and kisses his forehead*)
Pasmore Not bad.
Wendy Lifted the roof. It's a wonder you've a tile left on.

Pasmore That's your brother.
Wendy Not your wife?
Pasmore Could be her, an' all. (*He watches her*) Sleep in here, then, did you?

Wendy folds the blanket

Wendy That's right.
Pasmore Off in one or two minutes?
Wendy Correct.
Pasmore I used to get a kick out of that. Leaving the house. The three of you asleep. Your mother in bed. Sun rising. There's never once, going down, I didn't feel sick. Home-time, you'd see the colliers crawl in at the bottom: two minutes later, up top, they used to run. That glad to get out of it for ten or twelve hours. There we are, then. (*He claps his hands*) On with the dance!

Colin picks up the wine bottle from last night

Wendy (*indicating the bottle*) We had one or two drinks last night.
Pasmore Didn't know we had any.
Wendy Found it in the bottom of a cupboard. Forgotten you had it.
Pasmore That's right.
Colin I'll wash my hands. (*He goes out to the kitchen and puts the bottle in the waste-bin there*)
Wendy None of this misanthropy, Father.
Pasmore What's that?
Wendy Thinking that life has come to an end.
Pasmore It has.
Wendy That's misanthropy.
Pasmore Is it?
Wendy Or despair.
Pasmore I dreamt I met my brothers last night. Like we used to meet each Sunday.
Wendy Church?
Pasmore Evensong; door wide open, windows lit. Organ playing. (*Pause*) My mother wa' very religious. (*Pause*) If there isn't a God, we've certainly made a fine excuse for one.

Pause

Wendy Have you had any breakfast?
Pasmore Save up till lunchtime.
Wendy More tea?
Pasmore No thanks.
Wendy I'll talk to the shopkeeper.
Pasmore Will you?
Wendy When you go to the shop, let my mother go in, or, if you do go in, just watch yourself.
Pasmore I do nowt else. Don't worry. (*He looks up*) I'll go get washed.

He goes to the bathroom, passing Colin coming into the room from the kitchen

Act II, Scene 2

Pasmore goes into the bathroom and closes the door

Colin How is he?
Wendy Fine. You're not despairing, are you?
Colin No.

Mrs Pasmore's bedroom door opens. She comes out, dressed, with her walking-stick. There is daylight in the room behind

She takes a cup and saucer to the kitchen, rinses them under the tap, and looks round to tidy the room. She finds it tidy already

Wendy Relax.
Colin I am relaxed.
Wendy Odd meeting here like this.
Colin Yes.
Wendy Same flesh and blood.
Colin Yet different.
Wendy Right. (*She watches him*)

Pause

Mrs Pasmore pauses in the kitchen and contemplates going through to the living-room. She hesitates

What's she doing?
Colin Tidying.
Wendy You think so?
Colin Yes.

Mrs Pasmore hesitates with her hand on the kitchen door. She releases it as:

Eileen comes downstairs, briskly, noisily. She is dressed. She goes to the bathroom and finds it locked

Eileen Sorry! (*She comes into the living-room*) Sleep all right?
Wendy Splendid.
Eileen Breakfast?
Colin Had some.
Eileen Wendy?
Wendy No thanks.
Eileen Parents?
Colin Up.

Mrs Pasmore has "girded" herself. She opens the door and emerges

Eileen There you are, then, Mother.
Mrs Pasmore This is a surprise, finding you all here.
Wendy It is!
Eileen Slept well, I should think, after all that drink. (*She kisses her cheek*)
Mrs Pasmore Not that much, love. Though I did sleep well.
Eileen Anything I can get you?
Mrs Pasmore Colin brought me tea. That's all I have on a morning.
Eileen Can't face the world without something inside. (*She goes*)

Mrs Pasmore (*calling*) You'll find the food in the cupboard. And, if not in the cupboard, the fridge.

Pasmore emerges from the bathroom

Eileen 'Morning, Father!
Pasmore 'Morning, love.
Eileen All right?
Pasmore Champion.
Eileen Anything in the kitchen?
Pasmore No thanks. Empty, if you want. (*He indicates the bathroom*)
Eileen Right.

Eileen goes into the bathroom and closes the door

Pasmore (*to Mrs Pasmore*) They're leaving soon.
Colin Better get off early.
Mrs Pasmore Yes, love.
Wendy Best get off.
Pasmore Aye ... Right.

Pause. Pasmore sits

Wendy If I leave now, I may get back in time for my committee. (*To Pasmore*) I'll drop by at the shop.
Pasmore Right.
Wendy We'll sort it out.
Pasmore Aye.
Wendy Don't worry.

Pause. Wendy looks at Colin

Eileen comes out of the bathroom and goes through to the kitchen

I'll ring you both this evening.
Pasmore Right.
Wendy Goodbye, then, Dad. (*She kisses his cheek, stooping to him*)
Pasmore Goodbye, then, love. (*He allows his arms to be held*)
Wendy (*as Mrs Pasmore rises*) Goodbye, then, Mother. No need to get up.
Mrs Pasmore I'll get up, love.

They embrace, Mrs Pasmore almost formally, Wendy warmly

Wendy Bye, Colin.
Colin Bye, love.

They embrace and kiss each other's cheek

Wendy I'll say goodbye to Eileen in the kitchen.
Mrs Pasmore Right, then, love.
Wendy See each other more often.
Mrs Pasmore Yes.
Wendy (*after a pause*) Goodbye. (*She goes, without a backward glance, to the kitchen, taking her coat*)

Act II, Scene 2

Pasmore rises

Goodbye, our Eileen.
Eileen Are you off?
Wendy Just. (*She nods back to the living-room*)
Eileen I'll see you out.

They depart through the back door, Wendy drawing on her coat, Eileen following

In the living-room, Mrs Pasmore has gone to the window. Colin stands behind her, gazing out. Mrs Pasmore, after gazing out, turns away. She goes back to her chair. Pasmore goes to the window and gazes out

Pasmore Neat car.
Mrs Pasmore Has she?
Pasmore Didn't you see it?
Mrs Pasmore I did.
Pasmore (*waving*) She'll be asking Eileen to give her a shove. (*Pause*) There's Mrs who-is-it looking out next door.
Mrs Pasmore Which next door?
Pasmore Across the street.
Mrs Pasmore It's not a street.
Pasmore The road.
Mrs Pasmore She can't be next door if she's across the road.
Pasmore She's off. (*He waves, watches for a moment, then turns*)
Mrs Pasmore It's herself she's hurt more than anything else.
Colin She's gone to catch the shopkeeper, Mother.
Mrs Pasmore Has she?
Colin Before he opens up.
Pasmore She's given me my instructions.

Eileen comes in the back door. She feels the teapot, finds it hot, under the cosy, and pours a cup

Mrs Pasmore What are they, pray?
Pasmore I come to the door to carry your shopping.
Mrs Pasmore That's all you do at present.
Pasmore I shall go on doing it, in that case.
Mrs Pasmore I'll look forward to it, love.
Colin I dreamt last night that all this was a dream.
Mrs Pasmore It is.
Pasmore It doesn't feel like one. (*He sits*) "Our dream of life is o'er." Five letters. (*He indicates the newspaper*)

Pause

Mrs Pasmore I don't know love. (*She is abstracted*)

Pause

Eileen, having sipped her tea, comes through to the hall. She gets her coat and comes into the living-room

Eileen I'm off! Goodbye, Mother.
Mrs Pasmore (*rising*) Goodbye, love.

Eileen embraces her and kisses her cheek

Eileen I'll be over again quite shortly.
Mrs Pasmore Right, love.
Eileen Goodbye, Father.
Pasmore Goodbye, love.

He rises to be embraced. Eileen kisses his cheek

Eileen Cheerio, Colin.
Colin Cheerio.

She kisses and embraces him

Eileen (*to Mrs Pasmore*) I'll give you a call as soon as I'm back.
Mrs Pasmore Right, then, love.
Eileen I'll go the back way. Cheerio.

She goes, crossing the kitchen. She takes an apple from the bowl and puts it in her pocket. She closes the back door behind her

Mrs Pasmore goes to the window. Pasmore sits. Colin watches from behind Mrs Pasmore

Mrs Pasmore She always drove too fast.
Pasmore Always?
Mrs Pasmore Don't you remember how many goes she had to get her licence? (*She waves*) She almost took the gatepost off. (*Pause. She watches, then turns back to the room*) You left, Colin.
Colin Yes.

Mrs Pasmore sits

Mrs Pasmore Don't have to rush.
Colin No.
Mrs Pasmore You've a longer drive than either.
Colin I'd better make a start.
Mrs Pasmore Did you sleep any better last night? (*She gazes at him keenly*)
Colin I did. (*Pause*) I'll get my things.

He goes. He pauses outside the door, then continues upstairs

Mrs Pasmore You can turn off the drawer.
Pasmore Right. (*He gets up and moves the lever over the fire*)
Mrs Pasmore Burnt up.
Pasmore It has.
Mrs Pasmore Got the coal?
Pasmore Colin got it.
Mrs Pasmore You shouldn't have let him.
Pasmore Why not?
Mrs Pasmore That's your job.

Act II, Scene 2

Pasmore All my life.
Mrs Pasmore Don't feel so badly done to.
Pasmore I don't.
Mrs Pasmore I had such a funny dream last night. I dreamt I died. I called, "I'm dying". You were fast asleep.
Pasmore I dee'd as well.
Mrs Pasmore Is that what dying's like?
Pasmore Like what?
Mrs Pasmore Like waking from a sleep.

Pause

Colin comes down. He appears in his overcoat carrying a hold-all

Colin I've stripped the beds.
Mrs Pasmore Thank you, love. (*She stands and puts out her arms to be embraced*)
Colin Goodbye, Mother.
Mrs Pasmore Goodbye, love.

They hold the embrace for a moment. Then Colin kisses her on the cheek

Pasmore stands, looking on

Colin Goodbye, Dad.
Pasmore Goodbye, lad.

Colin embraces Pasmore

Colin Look after yourselves.
Pasmore We shall.
Colin I'll go out the back door: the front one's locked. Bye, then.
Mrs Pasmore Bye.

Colin goes out to the passage. He crosses the kitchen to the back door. He looks round at it briefly, glances towards the living-room, then goes, closing the back door behind him

You ought to have seen him off.
Pasmore I can see him off from here. (*He stoops to the window and waves*) Mrs who-is-it's out again.
Mrs Pasmore I wish you wouldn't call people something that they aren't.
Pasmore How do I know who she is? (*Pause. He waves*) He drives slower than our Wendy.

Pause. He watches a moment longer, then turns and comes back to the room

Mrs Pasmore Well, then.

Pause

Oh, now.

Pasmore shields his face

Oh, now. (*Not moving*)

Pasmore weeps

Oh, now, Tommy.

Pasmore, his face still shielded, is silent

Tell me—that time—when you marched in Russia.
Pasmore Russia.
Mrs Pasmore General Denisov.
Pasmore Denisov.
Mrs Pasmore He came aboard at Odessa.
Pasmore Odessa.
Mrs Pasmore In tears.
Pasmore In tears.
Mrs Pasmore With his wife.
Pasmore His wife.
Mrs Pasmore As the ship steamed out ...
Pasmore As the ship steamed out ...
Mrs Pasmore He took her hand.
Pasmore He took her hand. (*Pause*) He said. (*Pause*) "Oh where are we going to, my love?"

Her gaze, full of tears, is turned on her husband; his grief-stricken face is turned on hers. The anguish of their past and present life is evident between them

The light slowly fades

FURNITURE AND PROPERTY LIST

ACT I

Scene 1

On stage: Living-room
Fireplace with mantelpiece, tiled façade with metalwork, and drawing lever
Fireguard
Coal bucket with coal in it
Fire-irons
Rug in front of fire
Window with curtains
Three-piece suite with chair-covers, cushions, etc.
Clock (stopped) on mantelpiece
Sideboard with wine-glasses inside
Reading lamp
Coffee table
Television
Kitchen
Sink with functional tap
Electric stove (with practical light and clock)
Kitchen units with power-points, and cupboards containing cups and saucers, teapot, a vase, shoe-cleaning materials in a box, bottle of wine
Table (*with cloth*) and a tray bearing a teapot, teacups and saucers, sugar bowl, tea-bags, spoons
Kettle (practical)
Fruit bowl containing apples
Waste-bin
Window with curtains
Clock over electric stove
Refrigerator containing bottle of milk
Radio
Towel
Washing-machine
Back door with key, bolts and chain

Hall
Coat hooks
Pasmore's coat, hanging on hook

Personal: **Mrs Pasmore:** walking-stick

Scene 2

Strike:
Living-room
Coal bucket
Tray with cups and saucers, etc.

Set:	Cup on mantelpiece
	Newspaper
	Clock on mantelpiece now working
	Kitchen
Set:	On table: toast; plate; butter-dish; knife; teapot with tea in it; cup and saucer
Off stage:	Coal bucket with coal **(Pasmore)**
	Shoes **(Pasmore)**
	Coat and handbag **(Mrs Pasmore)**
	Handkerchief **(Mrs Pasmore)**
	Dark suit on hanger **(Pasmore)**
	Cup **(Colin)**
	Coat **(Colin)**
	Bunch of flowers **(Wendy)**
	Two cards and two telegrams **(Colin)**
Personal:	**Mrs Pasmore:** walking-stick, handkerchief, wristwatch
	Wendy: coat, handkerchief

ACT II

Scene 1

Off stage:	Box of chocolates **(Wendy)**
	Jeweller's box containing a ring **(Pasmore)**
Personal:	**Mrs Pasmore:** handkerchief
	Pasmore: handkerchief

Scene 2

	Living-room
Strike:	Coal in bucket (*leave empty bucket*)
Set:	Door open
	Blanket, over sleeping **Wendy**
	Wendy's coat
	Kitchen
Strike:	Dirty tea-things
Set:	Steaming kettle and pot of tea
	Clean cups and saucers
	Hall
Set:	**Eileen**'s coat
Off stage:	Coal **(Colin)**
	Walking-stick **(Mrs Pasmore)**
	Cup and saucer **(Mrs Pasmore)**
	Coat and hold-all **(Colin)**

LIGHTING PLOT

Practical fittings required; overhead lights in kitchen and living-room: reading lamp in living room

ACT I, SCENE 1

To open: Darkness. Glow from fire

Cue 1	A light goes on behind the closed door of **Pasmore**'s bedroom (Bedroom 1) *Snap up light in Bedroom 1*	(Page 1)
Cue 2	The light in Bedroom 1 goes off again *Snap off light in Bedroom 1*	(Page 1)
Cue 3	**Colin** puts on the reading lamp *Snap on covering spots*	(Page 2)
Cue 4	A light goes on behind **Mrs Pasmore**'s bedroom door (Bedroom 2) *Snap up light in Bedroom 2*	(Page 5)
Cue 5	**Pasmore** opens his bedroom door and switches on the light *Snap up Bedroom 1 light*	(Page 8)
Cue 6	**Pasmore** coughs from behind his bedroom door *Snap off light behind Bedroom 2 door. Snap off light behind Bedroom 1 door*	(Page 8)
Cue 7	**Colin** lies back *Light fades to black-out*	(Page 8)

ACT I, SCENE 2

To open: Morning

| Cue 8 | Wendy (*off*): "*Colin!*"
Light fades to black-out | (Page 34) |

ACT II, SCENE 1

To open: Evening: evening light at the living-room window, glow of the fire

| Cue 9 | **Eileen** switches on the living-room light
Snap up living-room light | (Page 35) |
| Cue 10 | **Mrs Pasmore** switches on the kitchen light
Snap up kitchen light | (Page 36) |

Cue 11	**Pasmore** goes into his bedroom (Bedroom 1) *Snap up light behind partially open door of Bedroom 1*	(Page 44)
Cue 12	**Mrs Passmore** goes into her room (Bedroom 2) and closes the door *Snap up light behind closed door of Bedroom 2*	(Page 44)
Cue 13	**All:** "Mother and Father". They drink *Light fades*	(Page 52)

ACT II, SCENE 2

To open: Morning. Shaded light in living room, stronger light in kitchen

Cue 14	**Wendy** draws open the living-room curtains *Flood living-room with "daylight"*	(Page 52)
Cue 15	**Pasmore** and **Mrs Pasmore** look at each other *Light slowly fades*	(Page 60)

EFFECTS PLOT

ACT I

Scene 1

Cue 1	A light goes on behind the door of Bedroom 2 *Noise of a knocked chair*	(Page 5)
Cue 2	**Mrs Pasmore** closes her bedroom door *Noise of a knocked chair; noise of a walking-stick*	(Page 7)

Scene 2

Cue 3	As Scene Two begins *The sound of a radio in the kitchen*	(Page 8)
Cue 4	**Mrs Pasmore** turns off the radio *Cut radio*	(Page 9)
Cue 5	**Pasmore:** "We have that in this house." *A bang overhead*	(Page 16)
Cue 6	They laugh *Tapping at front door*	(Page 22)
Cue 7	**Wendy**, having risen, glances about the room *Sound of bolts being drawn, a key turned, a chain released*	(Page 22)
Cue 8	**Pasmore:** "Nob'dy'll bloody believe it." *A bang at the front door*	(Page 24)
Cue 9	**Pasmore:** "Right!" *Sound of* **Colin** *coming downstairs*	(Page 33)
Cue 10	**Mrs Pasmore** leads the way to the front door *Sound of the front door opening*	(Page 33)
Cue 11	**Colin** exits *Sound of the front door closing and the key being turned*	(Page 34)

ACT II

Scene 1

Cue 12	As Act II begins *Sound of the front door being unlocked*	(Page 35)
Cue 13	**Mrs Pasmore:** "All he does is dirty it up." *Sound of front door closing*	(Page 37)

Scene 2

No cues

www.ingramcontent.com/pod-product-compliance
Ingram Content Group UK Ltd.
Pitfield, Milton Keynes, MK11 3LW, UK
UKHW021847210426
5322IPUK00022B/510